D1127061

The Priestly AMEN

countered many men older and wiser than I, many much holier than I, many much more learned than I. It has taken either a large amount of cheek or a fair amount of lunacy or more probably a considerable amount of both to stand before these men as their teacher or master—and that is precisely the role I assumed, for in each instance I came to them as their "retreat *master*." I did not face them without humility but I did face them without fear. What one knows he does not fear, and I know secular priests pretty well. For more than twenty-two years I have been living with them, working with them, playing and vacationing with them, listening to their gripes, hearing their confessions, counseling them in their troubles or going to them with my own—knowing the full gamut of their poor human weaknesses as well as the full splendor of their quiet but deep sanctity.

I know something of the hope and expectancy every priest brings to his annual retreat. I know that here at least he cannot tolerate more of the old pious platitudes—though he may be the first to admit that he himself is not above handing them out on occasion to others. I know that he comes to his retreat with a monumental hunger for real meat in the spiritual diet to be proffered him. How often he is disappointed almost to the point of retching! That is why I did not hesitate to wade into some rather deep theological waters in some of these talks, even at the conscious risk of wading in over my head. I am a parish priest and not a professional theologian. I know that any theologian who reads these talks will not have gone very far into them before he finds himself in wholehearted agreement with at least the second part of that statement. But I know too that my brothers in the secular priesthood want and need the good red meat of theological insight applied to their lives and work during their annual retreat. I did not presume myself theologically competent to do this, but for their sakes I was not afraid to try. My compassion for them outweighed my fear of theologians. So let the chips fall where they may!

The Priestly
AMEN

by Roy Rihn

SHEED AND WARD: NEW YORK

© Sheed and Ward, Inc., 1965

Library of Congress Catalog Card Number 65–12202

NIHIL OBSTAT
    Brendan Lawlor
    Censor Deputatus

IMPRIMATUR
    Patrick C. Brennan
    Vicar General, Diocese of Burlington
    October 13, 1964

Manufactured in the United States of America

Foreword

MUCH OF THE MATERIAL in this book is freely adapted from bo
and articles I have liked during several years of rather spor
reading. In fact, in certain instances the material is not-so-fr
adapted—it is all but bodily transferred. I regret that due ackn
edgement of this piracy is seldom made in the text. This reflect:
ill-concealed attempt to plagiarize. It simply reflects the fact
this was written for vocal delivery, and anyone who has ha
endure it knows that constant "name dropping" in a talk or ser
can be rather nettling. When these sermons were written there
neither faith nor hope on the part of the author that they w
ever see the light of day on the printed page. He therefore mac
special point of identifying the sources upon which he was dra
Permit me, then, to make amends in some measure here by ack
edging that much of what appears in the following pages I o
great and good men, living and dead, such as Louis Bouyer, J
Jungmann, A. M. Rouget, Charles Davis, Jean Danielou, E
Masure, Emile Guerry, Godfrey Diekmann, C. S. Lewis,
Rahner, F. X. Durrwell, Edward Schillebeeckx, et al.

These retreat talks were intended for the ears and the min
the great hearts of those men whom I know better than any
in all this world: secular priests. In coming before them

But my own theological incompetence was not the only problem. I know priests, and because I do I know that there is no horror like to their horror of sermons that are too long—when they, that is, are on the receiving end. Priests will forgive anything and everything about a sermon except its length. There is a kind of unwritten law in clergy retreats, a sort of assumed gentlemen's agreement, that none of the sermons shall last more than thirty minutes. Beyond this hallowed limit the retreat master may in rare instances be grudgingly allowed three or four additional minutes of grace, but beyond *that* he is a dead duck. For the retreat master, at times like this, over-simplification is not merely a convenient way out, it is a necessary means of survival. Would the kind reader of what follows, in a spirit of true empathy, please bear this in mind?

Roy Rhin
St. Pius X Rectory,
San Antonio, Texas

Contents

The Priestly AMEN

1. "I am the Lord thy God"—
God's Man and God

YOUR priestly life, Father, may be quite complex but it can be very simply stated. It is nothing more or less than an Amen. It is your Amen to God.

Our English language does not give us a word which corresponds exactly with this old Hebrew word "amen." It means acceptance, approval, ratification, commitment, surrender. Perhaps the closest we can come is the plain little word "yes," with all that that implies—and what it implies is staggering indeed.

In all of history there has been only one perfect Amen or Yes spoken by man to God, and the man who spoke it was God's own Son. "Thy will be done on earth as it is in heaven" he taught us to say—but he himself said "I have come down from heaven not to do my own will, but the will of him who sent me" (John 6:38). The "yes" of his redemptive death on the cross remains the one eternally perfect Amen of man to God. But this Amen is more than one man's Yes to God, because the man who spoke it is the head of redeemed mankind. He sent out his Spirit to incorporate you and me into himself, and he has thereby graciously involved you and me in this Amen. Your life and mine, most simply but most profoundly stated, is nothing more or less than our fumbling effort to join in his own great Amen.

In and through Christ, God has personally encountered each of us. He has made himself personally present to us, addressed us and called us by name. By the grace of God each of us can truly say, "The Lord called me from birth; from my mother's womb he gave me my name" (Isaias 49:1).

God's personal call to you is most marvelous indeed, for you he has called not merely into Christ's body but into Christ's priesthood. In his own way and in your particular situation God has presented himself in Person to you, spoken to you in the uttermost depths of your being, and called you by your eternal name which he alone knows. This personal presence and this personal call demand a response: *your* response. This response is your life—or rather, your life is this response. It is your Amen. Your Yes.

It is about some of the implications of this Amen or Yes that I want to talk to you in these pages.

The most obvious of these implications is that you must *involve* yourself. If God has made himself personally present to you, your first task is to make yourself personally present to him. The first implicate of God's meeting you is your meeting him. The first requisite of your response to God is simply that you encounter him.

Your initial reaction to this is probably that it presents nothing unusual or extraordinary. You will reply that you do this every day. You encounter God intimately and directly in the Mass, and especially in the Communion of the Mass. You encounter God's holy word daily in the Breviary. In the confessional you dispense God's pardon. In the baptistry you transmit his very life. Why then propose this as a unique purpose when it is already an everyday occurrence with you?

As a priest this *is* daily routine with you. Yes, as a priest. But what about you as a *person*? What about you as a man? How often do you-as-person encounter God-as-Person? How often do you meet him?

We enjoy two modes of encounter with God, both equally indispensable. First, we must meet God publicly, as his holy people, as his family the Church. This we do in the sacred liturgy—and in this confrontation you are privileged to act as president or leader. This kind of encounter you enjoy daily as a priest. But there is another mode of confrontation of at least equal importance. It is the completely personal encounter, the one that is strictly person-to-person. It is the encounter Martin Buber calls simply "I-Thou." In all candor, Father, how often do you as a man experience this kind of encounter with God?

The times in which we live conspire against true communication between persons. Even to begin speaking of someone in the third person as "he" is already to make of him something other than a real person. Without our realizing it, this "he" of whom we speak is to us already depersonalized: somehow just an object, a thing, an "it." This is possibly the *grand malaise* of our particular age with its accent on products and goods and gadgets and things, and underlies the pervading loneliness. Today the "I-thou" relation degenerates quickly into an "I-it" relation, involving an encounter not of true persons but of persons-considered-as-objects. This, Father, is our environment, described recently as "the age of the exuberantly growing It." We priests too are children of this depersonalized age. It leaves its mark upon our communication not only with *one another* as persons, but also with *God* as Person.

Schillebeeckx and others are pointing out to us that we have made an "it" of Grace and that we have quite depersonalized the Sacramental encounter. The "exuberantly growing It" has definitely invaded our religious experience. We priests who encounter God daily in our professional capacity can rock along for weeks or months without ever once encountering him truly person-to-Person.

God becomes merely part of the system. We speak to others about God, we point the way to him, we dispense his mysteries, we are the mediators between him and his people—and all the while *we* can neglect meeting *him,* person-to-person. Behold, *now* is the acceptable time.

Father, you must be convinced that you need this kind of deep and unabashedly personal communion with God. You must, in fact, be convinced that you cannot go on without it.

I shall say much less to you about the *how* of this encounter than about the *why. How* shall you find God? Perhaps the whole story of the *how* can be summed up by reminding you of something you say every day: *"nolite obdurare corda vestra"* (Psalm 94). You need do nothing more than do nothing to shut him out. For he is anything but disinterested. He is already seeking you—infinitely more intently than you could ever seek him. "It is not," says St. John, "as though we had loved God, but because He hath first loved us" (1 John 4:10). Your *search* for God will never be anything but a *response.* It is not so much a case of your having to seek him to discover him, as of your having simply to discover him seeking you!

And the *why:* why do you need to come into personal encounter with God?

Well first of all because I am only quoting *you.* You yourself say so, in touching and eloquent language, again and again throughout the week. Every Tuesday at Sext you say: "As the deer longs for the running waters, my soul, O God, longs for You! My soul thirsts for God, the God of my life" (Psalm 41:1–2). Every Sunday at Lauds you say: "O God, you are my God; with earnest care I seek You. My soul thirsts for You, my flesh hungers for You, as the parched and thirsty earth longs for water" (Psalm 62:1–2). Every Monday at Terce you say: "My heart speaks to You, O God; my face searches You out. I long, O Lord, for the sight of your face" (Psalm 26:8). More significant even than the fact that you say this is the fact that it is God who has you say it: these are his own words he puts upon your lips!

Another reason why you need to seek and find God, Father, is that it was precisely this need which accounts for your being a priest. You would not have become a priest had there not been a deep personal hunger for God in your heart as a young boy, as a young man. Don't be cynical about it, Father: that hunger is there still. With touching nostalgia you remind yourself that it is (or rather, God reminds you that it is) every morning as you begin Holy Mass: "Send forth your light and your truth; they have guided me and led me to your holy hill and to your dwelling. And I shall go in, to the altar of God, to the God who giveth joy to my youth" (Psalm 42:3-4, Mass version).

A third reason why you must intently seek *God* is that if you don't you shall probably end up seeking and finding only *yourself*. Isn't it true that so often we are completely preoccupied with self? We examine and ponder and analyse our faults and weaknesses and sins—the same poor tired faults and weaknesses and sins analysed and explored so often in the past, always with the same incipient hopes ending so quickly in the same humiliating defeat. The whole emphasis is on *me*. The preoccupation is with *self*. The pity of this is not so much its unhealthiness or its inevitable discouragement. The true pity of it is that in fixing our eyes so intently on self we never quite get around to raising them where they really belong: upon the great God our Father "who predestined us in love unto the adoption of children through Jesus Christ" (Eph. 1:5) ". . . and gave us everlasting consolation and good hope in grace" (II Thess. 2:16).

Sursum corda! Our hearts and our minds belong much more on God and much less on ourselves. Don't look so intently at yourself that you overlook God your Father who is the sole source of your hope. It is in *him* and not in self that you find salvation: He is "the God who saves." Our resolutions are so often tarred with this worn-out old Pelagian brush: they turn out to be glowing summations of what *I* will do rather than a hope of what God, through Grace, will enable me to do. *Quaerere Deum!* Do what every Tuesday at vespers you say you do: "To You I lift up my eyes, O God; to You who dwell in heaven. See, as the eyes of a maid-servant are on the hands of her mistress, so my eyes are on the Lord my God" (Psalm 122:1–2).

Finally and most compelling of all, you must seek God because you are his man. If Paul could say to the priest Timothy, I can say by equal right to you: you are "*homo Dei.*" How fortunate that we have opted "man of God" as the *popular* translation of "*homo Dei*" and therefore the meaningless one, because the other rendering, "God's man," is ever so much stronger. We haven't yet robbed that one of its meaning by making a cliché of it. *Father, you are God's man!* He called you and sent you to speak for him and about him. You are his prophet: you deliver his message. But not only do you make known to others what God *says;* in a unique manner you also make known to them who God *is.* Not only do you deliver his message: you also shape his image. This, inescapably, is your role as "*homo Dei.*" It is necessary therefore that you be in touch with God before you attempt to get in touch with God's people! You must not go to God's people except you come from the people's God!

This is the clear lesson of salvation history. Moses did not descend to the *qehal Yahweh* (the assembly of God's people) at the foot of the mountain, until first he had ascended the mountain to meet God in face-to-face encounter. Isaiah did not speak for God until the angel had touched the live ember to his lips. The stuttering and diffident Jeremiah dared go to God's people only after he had first met God in "I-Thou" encounter. Jesus, in immediate preparation for his role as prophet, must surely have had personal encounter not only with Satan but also with the Father during that retreat of his there in the desert. And Paul withdrew to the desert for "I-Thou" dialogue with God before setting out to bring God's good news to the people of the world.

Because you are *"homo Dei"* you not only tell men what God says, you also shape their image of who God is. The image of God you call forth in others cannot be other than the image of God already formed in yourself. What *is* that image, Father? I know of no question to put to you, God's man, more pressing or pertinent than this: "What think you of God?" It is you who are his man. What you think of him will have ever so much to do with what others think of him. I challenge you squarely with the question: "You, God's man, what think you of God?"

The late Cardinal Suhard wrote that a central problem of our age is our loss of the meaning of God. He did not mean loss of belief in God; he meant loss of a true concept of God by those who do believe in him. In his book on monasticism Father Bouyer says flatly that we have lost our sense of God because we have lost our sense of the holy. God did indeed make man in his own image, but in our time it would appear that man has made God in his image. We have cut God down to our own size. We have portrayed him as our co-pilot, as our big buddy, as our comrade, as "the man upstairs." We do not deny that he exists, but the impression we give is that he exists only to help and console us. God may still be in his heaven, but we regard him as there precisely and exclusively for the service and use of man.

We have vulgarized his holiness and demeaned his sovereign majesty with an offensive sentimentalism which mocks his meaning. Many of our more thoughtful atheists do not really deny *God*—what they reject is this parody of God modern man has erected in place of the true God. One of these men, writing in *Harper's,* poked sly fun at the whole thing: *"Modern Screen Magazine,"* he said, "ran a series of articles called 'How the Stars Found Faith.' They included Piper Laurie's account of a day during her visit to Korea when she was riding back through the enemy patrols. And Piper wrote: 'I felt wonderful because I knew, somehow I just knew, there were not four of us but five of us going back in that jeep. And guess who the fifth passenger was. It was good old God.' And Jane Russell spoke up for God too: 'I love God. And when you get to know him, you find he's a Livin' Doll'." No doubt you have observed the religious jags which periodically overwhelm our popular song writers. Put another nickel in, in the nickel-o-deon—and get religion, learn all about God! Of course we must confess that some of our vernacular Catholic hymns are almost as bad: "O God of loveliness . . . So sweet thy countenance." And what of the tawdry sentimentalism encountered in some of our popular Catholic "prayer books?" Ah yes, "some of our most horrible blasphemies are those we utter on our knees."

Father, you are God's man. You are his prophet. How seriously has this modern caricature of God eroded your own concept of God? What think *you* of God? And have you here or there unwittingly added a stroke or two to the caricature? As God's man you have no trust more sacred or duty more primary than to communicate, by everything you say and do and are, a sense of the transcendent holiness and majesty of God.

What think you of God? To think right, go to the Scriptures, for as Pascal said, "God speaks well of God." What do you find there? What does *God* say about God?

That he is THE Lord. He is sovereign. He IS. "The earth is the Lord's and the fullness thereof, the world and all they that dwell therein" (Psalm 23:1) ". . . I am the Lord, and there is none other; there is no god besides me" (Isaiah 45:5) ". . . I am the Lord thy God, mighty, jealous" (Exodus 20:5) ". . . I am who am; tell them 'He who IS' sent you" (Exodus 3:14).

He is a hidden God. "Verily," said Isaiah, "thou art a hidden God" (Isaiah 45:15). He is, according to Paul, the God who "dwells in unapproachable light (whom) no man has ever seen or ever can see" (1 Tim. 6:16).

He is terrible, awesome. "Show me thy face that I may know thee," pleaded Moses. "Thou canst not see my face: for no man can look upon Me and live," was his reply (Exodus 33:18-20). "It is a terrible thing," says the author of Hebrews, "to fall into the hands of the living God ... Let us worship God as he would have us worship him: in awe and reverence" (Heb. 10:31 and 12:28).

He is the infinite God. "Can you find out the nature of God," asks the Book of Job. "It is higher than heaven, what can you do? Deeper than hell, what can you know? The measure thereof is longer than the earth and broader than the sea" (Job 11:7-9).

Above all he tells us that he is "the holy God." "I am the Lord thy God, the Holy One of Israel" (Isaiah 43:3). Always and everywhere, even in heaven, the approach to him is inescapably adoration; for St. John tells us in the Apocalypse that even the mighty Seraphim "cry out night and day without ceasing: 'Holy, holy, holy is the Lord God Almighty'" (Apoc. 4:8). Have you ever thought of this? Whatever our attempt at describing God, this is the very best we can do: to say "God is holy." What we mean by this is that he is completely "other," that he is utterly apart. For the real meaning of the word "holy" or "sacred" is precisely this: that which is apart. To say "God is holy" is to admit that in speaking of him we are frustrated before we begin, because he is so apart and so "other" from us that all our human words and symbols and concepts fail utterly. In trying to describe God every resource is ultimately stripped from us except the stark naked negative: God is holy—that is, he is the Completely Other, the Infinitely Apart.

The mystery of mysteries is that *this* God desires communion with us. He to whom we cannot go, comes to us! What is most difficult to believe about God is not that he is, or that he is infinite, but that *he is in love with the likes of us! The* mystery about God is this: the holy and terrible God who came to Sinai in blinding lightning and rolling thunder, dealing death to any man daring to touch even the mountain, the God upon whom no man can look and live—*this* is the God who is the loving, doting Father who watches for the prodigal's return and who runs down the road to throw his arms around him in exuberant embrace. He is "our Father who art in heaven" (Matt. 6:9) ". . . the merciful Father who gives all consolation" (II Cor. 1:3). He is the same God who "has so shown his love towards us that we should be called his sons and should be his sons" (1 John 3:1). And "to prove that we are sons, he has sent out the Spirit of his Son into our hearts, crying out in us 'Abba, Father' " (Gal. 4:6).

The true magnificence of the "gift of God" of which Jesus spoke to the Samaritan woman at Jacob's well is not merely that it is a gift which God himself *makes* to us, but that it is the gift by which God *gives himself* to us. Grace is first and foremost the *self-gift* of God. Ultimately Grace is God himself—not the created grace but the Uncreated Grace, not something but Some One! "If a man has any love for me . . . he will win my Father's love and we will both come to him and make our continual abode with him" (John 14:23).

"God speaks well of God," and we note that when he speaks most intimately about himself, what he tells us is not that he is the awesome God who created man but the tender God who cares for man: "I, the Lord, am your God who brought you out of the land of Egypt, that place of slavery" (Exodus 20:2); "I am the Lord who brought you from Ur in Chaldea to give you this land to possess" (Genesis 15:7).

"God speaks well of God," and perhaps nowhere has God spoken more eloquently of his love for man than in the Book of the Prophet Osee. Osee was one of those rare men capable of loving a woman completely. He loved and married the beauteous Gomer. But after the birth of their third child she left him and became a common whore. Osee's heart broke but his love never wavered. However, this man's love was truly extraordinary: it was not merely the kind that forgives, it was the kind that redeems. Osee's love was so strong, so virile, that he knew it would go out from himself to touch this wanton woman even in her sins and transfigure her, blot out all her wickedness and bring her back to him as whole as though she had never broken faith with him. And, you know, he was right! It did! He was this kind of tremendous lover.

Osee's wracking personal experience is what gives poignancy and power and truth to his revelation about God. It was inside his own heart that this man discovered and then revealed to us the kind of love God has for us. It is not the kind that merely forgives; it is the kind that redeems. Not only is it a constant, unyielding, never-say-die love. It is a healing love—a redeeming love so strong and active it transfigures the beloved even in his unfaithfulness. God's love is not merely the kind that waits until we have ceased being unjust in order to love us. He loves us already in our unjustness. As St. Paul put it: "It is in this that God has shown the greatness of his love for us: that his Son died for us while we were still sinners" (Rom. 5:8–9). And the reason why God does not wait for us to be loveable before loving us is precisely that his love is the only force that can make us loveable at all! It is only God's love for us that makes us worthy of his love!

Osee switches metaphors in the eleventh chapter of his book and, in place of the marriage figure, he substitutes the figure of a father's love for his infant son to reveal the true quality of the divine "*hesed*." Father, I don't know about you, but I find that I am strangely and profoundly touched at Sunday Mass when I see my people coming to the Communion table with their babies in their arms. But most especially moving is the sight of the men, the fathers, bearing their infant children in their arms. Perhaps this affects me so deeply because it is a joy I have personally never known. But whatever the reason, there is something that claws at my heart-strings when I see a father with his young son cradled in his arms.

Osee had three children of his own. So when this sensitive man wanted to deepen our insight into the fuller beauty of God's love for us, he used this figure of a father holding his infant son in his

arms. In what is certainly one of the most daring passages in all of
the Bible, he has God say: "When (my chosen people) Israel was
a child I loved him. Out of Egypt I called my son. It was I who
taught them to walk, who took them in my arms. I drew them with
human cords, with bands of love. I fostered them like one who
raises an infant to his cheeks" (Osee 11:1-4).

"God speaks well of God." What does he tell us about himself?
That he is the Lord God? Mighty and awe-inspiring? He who IS?
The Holy One of Israel? Yes. But more than that. He tells us too
that he is our Father whose patient love teaches us to take our first
toddling steps toward him, who sweeps us up into his strong protec-
tive arms and cuddles us to his cheek!

Yes, this is the real mystery about God: he is the Completely
Other, yet he makes his abode with us. He is the hidden God who
dwells in unapproachable light, yet he reveals himself to us and in
fact gives himself to us. He is the Utterly Apart, yet he is near, so
intimately near that he snuggles us to his cheek.

He is the God who calls to *you*, Father. He is The Holy One, the
transcendent God whom you dare approach only in awe and reverence. But he calls you and seeks you. He loves you. He yearns for
personal communion with you. He wants to "foster you like one
who raises an infant to his cheeks." "Today if you hear his voice,
harden not your heart" (Psalm 94:7-8). Father, don't be like that
unhappy man about whom you read every Tuesday at Matins in
the 37th psalm: "I have become like the man who is unable to
hear and who finds no response on his lips" (Psalm 37:15). Father,
now, use those ears of yours which were opened to his call at
Baptism. Hear that call—it is addressed to you still. Let there be a
response on your lips and in your heart. Say "yes" to him.

2. "His great love for man"—
Remembrance and Thanksgiving

SOMEWHERE I READ recently that "man's greatest need is the need of thanksgiving." It is even more to the point to say that the *Christian* man's greatest need is the need of thanksgiving. For the Christian, be he layman or priest, religion *begins* with thanksgiving. Absolutely nothing is more basic or more indispensable to authentically Christian piety than the spirit and act of thanksgiving. And if someone wiser than I were to tell us what is the one thing most awry with Catholic spirituality today, he might very well single out the deemphasis of thanksgiving which has quietly occurred among us. And if what I am saying here strikes you as wildly implausible I shall have made my point: it is a fact that in our time we do not regard thanksgiving as of really first-rate importance. We neither understand it nor appreciate its place in the Christian life.

It was not always thus. Time was when Christians knew better. This is obvious from the New Testament, for it is shot-through with an irrepressible spirit of thanksgiving. And of course the New Testament merely picks up and brings to full climax the crescendo of thanksgiving begun in the Old. The New Testament does not inaugurate salvation history—it completes it. The spirit of thanksgiving which burst into full glory in the New Testament's "fullness of time" had been building up and gathering force for hundreds of years. The Old Testament is not merely the account of the "*mirabilia Dei*," it is also the loving and living remembrance of these saving acts of God expressed in a sublime spirit of thanksgiving. "Giving thanks" is the inner genius of the Old Testament liturgy; it is the grand theme of many of the Psalms; it is the keynote of the great Prophets. But it is only in the definitive "*mirabilia Dei*" of the New Testament that thanksgiving reaches full estate. It is the man of the New Covenant, even more than the man of the Old Covenant, who senses this ineluctable compulsion to "give thanks." It is the *Christian* man whose deepest religious need is the need of thanksgiving. The writings of the New Testament reflect this. Thanksgiving is a theme that runs through the letters of St. Paul like an unending refrain. As you read those letters you come across the expression "giving thanks to God" or its equivalent more than forty times. Paul summed up his whole ascetical theology in one short sentence in Second Thessalonians when he wrote: "We ought to give thanks to God always." And we note that Jesus himself took the same approach: he gave thanks to his Father immediately before multiplying the loaves and fishes (John 6), immediately before raising Lazarus from the dead (John 11), and immediately before instituting the Holy Eucharist. Of course you readily recognize the very word "eucharist" as significant: it means "thanksgiving." What is even more significant is that this is one of the oldest and to this day still the official title given the great Sacrifice-Sacrament which is the very center of our Christian life. It should strike us as odd that today this title strikes us as odd. It should give us pause that we today regard "thanksgiving" such a strange and apparently inappropriate title to give to the Mass and Communion.

Perhaps we fail to notice thanksgiving's pride of place in the Mass itself. The Preface is thanksgiving. One of the more unfortunate twists of semantics is that our word "preface" now suggests a mere prelude or prologue, a kind of introductory device which is not too important in itself. We are tempted to take this impression of the Preface of the Mass. And unfortunately, the present arrangement of the Roman Missal adds to this impression by physically separating the Preface from the Canon. The arrangement is familiar to you. There is the section containing the sixteen prefaces now in our Missal; then you turn to the highly ornate page beginning with the cross-like T of the "*Te Igitur*" introducing the Canon. (These prefaces, by the way, had proliferated enormously until there were literally hundreds of them in use at the time of St. Pius V. Thanks to his reform of the Missal, all but about a dozen were mercifully eliminated. There is ground for suspicion, however, that this reform, so welcome in so many respects, may have "thrown out the baby with the bath" because the Prefaces we now have are not exactly the finest examples of classical Christian thanksgiving, and two of them are not thanksgivings at all: the Preface of the Trinity is a creed and the Preface of the Apostles is a petition.)

The point, however, is that our Missal today separates the Preface from the Canon. Actually they belong together. Etymologically this word "preface" means something spoken aloud before an assembly. Liturgically it means something of such importance that it has to be spoken aloud before the assembly of God's people. Historically the Preface is the beginning of the great "eucharistic prayer," the Mass itself. It is significant that this is the only part of the great Eucharistic Prayer to have survived the tyranny of silence which gradually enveloped the rest of the Canon. Throughout its history, from the Last Supper to this day, the Mass, focal point of our Christian worship and wellspring of our Christian sanctification, formally begins with a rousing summons to thanksgiving: "Lift up your hearts . . . Let us *give thanks* to the Lord our God . . . It is in very truth fitting and just and right and salutary to *give thanks* at all times and in all places to Thee, the Lord, holy Father, almighty and eternal God . . ." What strong and laboriously specific language! It occurs not in some pious book, but is accorded pride of place at the very heart and center of the liturgy itself. The Church could not have found a more prestigious spot in which to say this or a more favored setting in which to place it. She has reserved center stage to tell and remind us, day after day, of the unique importance of thanksgiving. We have got to sit up and take notice!

Perhaps it were not amiss to pause at this point and ask: "What precisely is "thanksgiving?" What does "giving thanks" really mean?" Shakespeare, that master of insight, went straight to the heart of the matter when he said, "Evermore thanks, the exchequer of the poor" (Richard II, II:3). To give thanks means to admit that you are poor. It is to imply that you are deeply aware of having received a favor which you cannot repay. In fact, to give thanks is to imply more than that you are poor: it is to imply that you are completely poor and cannot repay. When you *can* repay, then the thing to do *is* to repay, or at least to give something in exchange or in compensation. When none of these is possible, the one, the only recourse left is to give thanks. When you cannot *give anything,* then you *give thanks.* To give thanks to God means two things: an awareness that we owe everything to him, and an awareness that we cannot repay him for it. It is only when you lay full hold upon the great truth that you cannot repay God that you will appreciate the only alternative left: to give thanks to God. Christian thanksgiving is this two-fold admission-in-faith: a deep awareness of our indebtedness to him and of our utter incapability of repaying him. Is anything more basic to Christianity than this? It is nothing more or less than a recognition, in the practical order, of the whole theology of the gratuity of grace, of divine adoption, of the Redemption itself. It is the indispensable first step in true Christian piety. It is the corner-stone of Catholic spirituality—for the layman and for the priest.

But somehow we do not see this today. The beginning of the Preface sounds, at best, just slightly hyperbolic to us. Why? Why does thanksgiving not loom as fundamental in the Christian life as it should or as it once did? Because we do not *remember*. Not giving thanks is the price we pay for not remembering. To begin to understand and appreciate the place of thanksgiving in the Christian life means simply to begin to remember. To remember what? To remember that our God is "the Lord of history." To remember that "our God is the God who saves" and that we should be surely lost had he not acted to save us. It is to remember the gospel, the Good News of redemption wrought by God's son.

And "remember" is the right word. It is not just the story of the redemption but the history of the redemption. Christianity is essentially an historical religion. It rests not upon any completely "other worldly" phenomenon but upon the solid historical fact that Jesus Christ, eternal Son of God, sent in the fulness of time by his Father's love, came into this world as man and redeemed us. This he did at a definite point in time and space. "When the fulness of time came," said Paul, "God sent his own Son, born of a woman, born under the law, to be a ransom for those who were subject to the law and to make us sons by adoption . . . No longer then art thou a slave, thou art a son. And because thou art a son thou hast the son's right of inheritance" (Gal. 4). It is a fact of history that God so loved the world that he sent his only-begotten Son into it to redeem it by his death and resurrection. Not only the *least* thing we *can* do, but the *first* thing we *must* do, is simply to *be aware* of this—to remember it! When we do, we shall realize that we had nothing to do with it, that we did not "merit" it, that we cannot repay it. And then we *will* give thanks.

This is why the great Thanksgiving, the Mass, is an act of remembrance. Ever since the Reformation we have been so busy defending the truth that the Mass is a sacrifice that we have all but forgotten that it is also a memorial. Yet it *is* that, first and foremost, because when our Lord gave us the Mass he assigned no other reason for it than this! "Do this," he said. "Offer the Mass." Yes, but

why? "Do this IN MEMORY OF ME." Indeed there are other
reasons for celebrating the Eucharist, for doing what the Lord did
at the Last Supper—but it is worthy of note that *remembrance* is the
only reason Jesus himself explicitly ascribed. The Eucharist is indeed a sacrifice, but first of all it is a memorial, it is an occasion for
remembering something. That is why, in the very act of confecting
the sacrifice, you say: "*Haec quotiescumque feceritis in mei memor-
iam facietis*—Every time you do this, you are to do it in remembrance of me." Appropriately enough, the very next thing you then
do *is* to remember. Immediately after the Consecration there follows
the *anamnesis,* the Christian community's great solemn act of
remembrance: "Wherefore, O Lord, we, thy ministers and thy holy
people, REMEMBERING the blessed passion . . . resurrection and
glorious ascension of Christ thy Son . . . " It is only after you say
"*Unde et memores*" that you say "*offerimus.*" You and the people of
God assembled around you ("*nos, servi tui et plebs tua sancta*")
pause to remember. Individually and communally you recall to
mind the central historical facts of the redemption. You remember
how God loved you. You remember the saving acts of God in
Christ. It is essential to your Christian Faith that you do this. Your
Christian Faith takes its origin, humanly speaking, from this remembrance: a remembrance which can issue only in the joyous
response of thanksgiving.

This daily exercise in remembering occasioned by Holy Mass is
meditation material of the highest order. It even comes equipped
with the "three points" of which the authors of meditation manuals
are so enamored: passion, resurrection, ascension. Unfortunately it
is said and done with in a flash and, of course, the rubrics do not
allow us to take a "time out" at this point for personal meditative
reflection. And let each of us confess and not deny: there are times
when it is not only not a meditation, it is not even the barest remembrance, for our poor sleepy or distracted minds do not even
consciously advert to the Lord's passion, resurrection and ascension

during the precious few seconds our lips so piously allege that we do remember. May I therefore make with you this meditation suggested daily by the Mass we offer?

We tell the Father first that we remember the "blessed" Passion of "the same Christ your Son our Lord." This should be a reflective remembrance: a recalling to mind not so much of the *what* as of the *why*. This remembrance should not be frittered away on that peculiar and suspicious dalliance over the gruesome details of the Lord's sufferings and death which became the vogue in the later Middle Ages and continues to this day. There is something unhealthy about this grim obsession with the details of the bloody sweat, scourging, crowning with thorns, crucifixion and death agony. This is not Sacred Scripture's way of remembering the Passion. Those two great New Testament "theologians of the Passion," the Apostles Peter and Paul, nowhere in their numerous references to the passion and death of Jesus ever descend to descriptive details. Invariably they mention only the barest facts and proceed immediately to what lies behind the facts. Even the four gospel accounts of the Passion, while more detailed here than anywhere else, are notably unencumbered. Compared to the lurid flights encountered in some of our pious books or *Tre Ore* oratory, Matthew, Mark, Luke and John are positively Spartan. The early Church always spoke of the "beata *Passio*"—and so, incidentally, does the Mass.

Our remembrance of the Passion, then, should devolve not so much around the *what* of the Lord's sufferings but rather around the *why*. St. Peter is a trustworthy guide. This is the way he remembered: "Christ suffered for our sakes . . . On the cross his own body took the weight of our sins . . . It was his wounds that healed you . . . Christ died as a ransom, paid once for all, on behalf of our sins: he the innocent for us the guilty, so as to present us in God's sight." (First Epistle of the Blessed Apostle Peter, passim) And this is the way St. Paul remembered: "Christ was handed over to death for our sins . . ." "We were reconciled to God through his Son's death and, so reconciled, we are surer than ever of finding salvation" (Rom. 4:25 & 5:10).

This should be the pattern of our remembering too: "Christ suffered *for our sakes* . . . He was handed over to death *for our sins* . . . *His* body took the weight of *our* sins . . . He who knew not sin was made into sin for us that we might be turned into the holiness of God . . . Christ died as a ransom for our sins: he the innocent for us the guilty." This is the way the New Testament "remembers" the Lord's sufferings and death: no sadistic savoring of the details but a mere mention of the fact in order to proceed straightaway to the glorious truth behind the fact.

To follow Scripture's lead in your remembrance of Christ's passion and death is also to be aware of what it accomplished: "We were reconciled to God through his Son's death . . . Christ died as a ransom, paid once for all, on behalf of our sins." What a simple and unequivocal statement this is, but how difficult for us to accept— really and truly accept. It is all but impossible for us Catholics, priests and people, to rid ourselves of the subtly conceited and erroneous notion that somehow *we* atone for our sins. Somehow God's word to us fails to penetrate our thick Pelagian hides. Somehow we cannot come to terms with the simple assertion that the ransom paid once and for all for our sins is the death of Jesus. Somehow we cannot really accept the statement that we are reconciled to God, not through any efforts of ours, but "through his Son's death." Perhaps if we priests show the way in "remembering" this, our people will follow.

We also tell the Father that we remember "the resurrection of the same Christ your Son our Lord." But do we? Father, if anything needs to be remembered in the Church today it is the resurrection of the Lord. For centuries now, we in the Western Church have not really remembered it. Only now, thanks to the insights of men like Durrwell and Lyonnet, are we beginning again to discover its

real meaning and true importance. For so very long we hardly knew
what to do with this mystery, relegating it at best to the merely
apologetic role of proving the divinity of Christ. How this has
impoverished us, and with what a truncated view of the Redemption it has saddled us! We see the Redemption largely, if not
exclusively, in terms of the Lord's *death*. To us today the Redemption means simply atonement for sin. The emphasis of our piety, of
our remembering, has focused on the crucifixion and ignored the
resurrection. We are indeed aware that Christ saved us by his
death, but we are not as deeply aware that he saved us by his
resurrection too. We are "crucifixion Christians" but we are not
"resurrection Christians." You can tell just from the way we furnish
and decorate our churches. Often our altars are dominated by huge,
larger-than-life representations of the dead, crucified Christ. The
"stations of the Cross," preoccupied exclusively with the passion
and ending abruptly with the burial, form a major (and sometimes
dominant) architectural and artistic feature of the interior. But
where is there any hint or suggestion or reminder of the resurrection? The suffering, crucified Christ? The dead Christ? Yes. But
the victorious, risen Christ? The living Christ? As a rule, completely
ignored—except for the dear little paschal candle!

This is significant. And it is wrong. I am not suggesting that it is
wrong to place reminders in our churches of the Lord's passion and
death. By all means let us keep them. But I do say that something
is awry when we completely ignore his resurrection.

It is disastrous theology to separate Christ's death from his resur-
rection-ascension. All three constitute the *one* Paschal Mystery. The
Church does not separate them. She took centuries to develop
separate observances of Good Friday and Ascension Thursday as
distinct from the Resurrection. For a very long time Easter Sunday
was the one feast of the one paschal mystery, and every Sunday was
a "little Easter." Even now the Church does not separate them. In
her liturgy on Good Friday she prays: "We adore your Cross, O

Lord, and we praise and glorify your holy Resurrection, for behold by that wood joy came into the world." Daily in the Mass the Church remembers the resurrection and ascension in the same breath with the passion.

At the conscious risk of oversimplification, and at the larger risk of conceptually fragmentizing the one paschal mystery which constitutes the one objective act of Redemption, for our purposes here let me say that there are TWO aspects to the Redemption. Atonement for sin is one aspect—but only one. The other is that Christ elevated man to share God's life. He accomplished the one by his passion and death. He accomplished the other by his resurrection which established him "Son of God in power" (Romans 1:4) and empowered him to send the Holy Spirit. In that key statement in Romans, Paul says not only that Jesus our Lord "was handed over to death for our sins," but adds immediately "and was raised to life for our justification" (Romans 4:25). In the magnificent Easter Preface which you proclaim day after day throughout Paschaltide you give thanks to the Father for the saving act of the true Lamb of God "who by dying destroyed our death, and by rising restored our life—*qui mortem nostram moriendo destruxit, et vitam resurgendo reparavit.*" It is indeed necessary for us to remember that Jesus atoned for our sins by his passion and death. But we had better remember also that atoning for our sins was by no means *all* he did for us. He also raised us to life!

Christianity is more than the bare removal of sin, and to be a Christian means more than to be without sin. The crux of the "good news" is that God so loved us that we are not merely *called* his sons but *are* his sons (I John 3:1). To be a Christian means above all to share God's life. Now how and why do we do that? Precisely and only because the man who is God's only-begotten Son arose from the dead. We participate in the divine life because the resurrection enabled Jesus Christ to send out his Spirit to incorporate us into the living body of the Risen Christ. We have got to see

Christianity not merely as the *absence* of something but as the *presence* of something: the presence in us of the divine life, a sharing through Christ in God's life. Nay, we have got to see Christianity not merely as the presence in us of *something,* but as the presence in us of *Some One:* the outpouring and indwelling of the Holy Spirit (John 14:16–17); the presence in us of both the Father and the Son who not only come to us but who make their continual abode with us (John 14:24). This means that we have got to remember the Lord's resurrection and restore it to its central place in the Redemption: to see it once again in proper perspective as the definitive salvific act of God. Truly to understand what adoptive sonship means, and fully to appreciate what God did for us, we must remember the resurrection.

Finally, we tell the Father every morning at Mass that we remember "the glorious ascension into heaven of the same Christ your Son our Lord." We remember that he found his way to the Father. Not only do we remember that this happened, but also, and very especially, should we remember what it means. And what does it mean? Quite simply that *we too* are going to heaven—that we too are going to find *our* way to the Father. Because *Christ* ascended into heaven *we* will too, because we are bodily united with him. As Pope St. Leo puts it in that great sermon which the Church has us read in our breviaries on the feast of the Lord's Ascension: where the Head of the body is, there will the rest of the body be too. St. Paul states it even more boldly: "With what an excess of love God loved us! Our sins had made dead men of us, and he, in giving life to Christ (by the resurrection), gave life to us too . . . raised us up too, enthroned us too above the heavens, in Christ Jesus" (Ephesians 2:5–6). So literally does Paul regard our unity with Christ that he can speak with utter aplomb of our actual enthronement in glory as a *fait accompli!*

Remembering the historical fact of the Lord's ascension tells you not only *why* you are going to heaven but also *how* you shall go

there. He himself told you. Listen again to his electrifying dis-
closure at the Last Supper: " 'In my Father's house there are many
mansions. Were it not so I should have told you, because I go to
prepare a place for you. And if I go and prepare a place for you, I am
coming again and I will take you to myself, that where I am, there
you also may be. Where I go you know, and the way you know.'
Thomas said to him, 'Lord, we do not know where thou art going,
and how can we know the way?' Jesus said to him: 'I am the way,
and the truth and the life. No one comes to the Father except
through me' " (John 14:1-6). Notice that: "I am the way . . . No
one comes to the Father except through me."

To remember the Lord's ascension is also to confront the fact
that the *man,* Jesus Christ, is enthroned in glory at the Father's right
hand: not just this man's soul but his body too—*HE* is there! If, as
St. Paul assures us, we, the real "we," are to be enthroned too above
the heavens in Christ Jesus, it should be worth remembering that
this marvelous hope applies not just to the "ascension" of our *souls.*
Really to remember the mystery of the Lord's ascension means to
leap beyond the confines of our peculiar Catholic syndrome of
"saving the soul." The redemptive purpose of the paschal mystery
was not to save your soul—it was to save *you.* You are you and I am
I and your soul is not you and my soul is not me and you will
pardon my grammar but not my statement. "I am coming again
and I will take *you* to myself, that where I am there *you* also may
be." The true vision of our Christian faith and the full expanse of
our Christian hope does not stop dead at the salvation of our *souls.*
Our hope and expectation is that we, the real we, real men who are
body and soul, will be "enthroned above the heavens in Christ
Jesus." We know that this finalizing of our Christian hope must be
deferred to "that day" promised by him when he said "*I am coming
again* and I will take you to myself." Really to remember the Lord's
ascension is to be aware of and alive to the *Parousia*—the end time
when the real "we," all of us gathered together into him who is the

way, return to the Father. In a certain sense we have our tenses
mixed up about the Lord's ascension into heaven: not past but
future: it *has* not happened, it *will* happen. In a certain sense the
Christ will have truly ascended into heaven only when the *whole*
Christ, Head and members, is enthroned in glory. Christ's *whole*
body is not yet ascended. Only when he "comes again" shall it be.
But it is *we* who are his body; it is not our souls which are his body.
Not just our souls but we are to be "enthroned above the heavens
in Christ Jesus." *This* is our Christian hope. But the pledge and
guarantee of this hope is our remembrance of his ascension. For it
is the presence in glory of "one of us," a man, the man Jesus Christ
who is also God, which is the seed of our hope that we too shall be
there—not merely as disembodied human souls but as real and true
human beings.

Unde et memores! Nothing is more basic to the religion of the
Christian than that he recall to mind the definitive saving acts of
his God: the blessed passion, resurrection and glorious ascension of
Jesus Christ. The first and indispensable step in true Christian piety
is to raise our eyes to the God who saves and remember what he did.
To each of us his own must be those lines of Psalm 122: "To You I
lift up my eyes, to You who dwell in heaven; see . . . as the eyes of a
servant are fixed on the hands of her mistress, so our eyes are on
the Lord our God."

Do we not find here the cause of so much that is so wrong with
our Catholic spirituality today? Our eyes are *not* on God. We do
not remember. Our eyes are turned inward upon ourselves. At heart
we are practicing Pelagians. A conceited kind of "do-it-yourself"
spirituality is all the vogue. The fashionable preoccupation is with
merit rather than with grace which alone accounts for merit. Our
spirituality starts with self, not with God. The accent is on what I
do rather than on what God has done. Personal responsibility re-
places personal response. We are engrossed in our own efforts to
win salvation—fascinated with self in a strange kind of religious

narcissism. We talk entirely too much about "acquiring virtue," with the obvious implication that virtue is some sort of skill we acquire by dint of personal effort, like good handwriting or a well-grooved golf swing. We hear over and over about "spiritual exercises," as though Christian sanctity, like slimming the waistline or building big muscles, can be reduced to a system of personal exercises whose initiative (if not whose results) depends on ourselves. We are not even averse to including some of the sacraments in this tidy little program of push-button spirituality. What is most devastating about all this is our bald insistence on private enterprise as the key to success.

Sursum Corda! Lift up your hearts! Have you lifted them up as you say you have: *ad Dominum?* It is there, all the way there, you are to raise them: beyond self to the God who saves, *"ad Dominum."* Raise the blinds! Let in God's glorious light! Open the window! Let in the fresh air of the Spirit! In short, remember. Remember what God did to save and redeem mankind. Remember the blessed passion, resurrection and glorious ascension of his Son our Lord, Jesus Christ. Remember his sending of the Holy Spirit. Remember the sacraments: the primordial sacrament, the Church, and the seven others. It is from these we draw our spirituality. It was to these essential mysteries of our faith St. Pius X pointed as "the primary and indispensable sources of the Christian spirit." Remember this. Be aware of it. Then, in your humble amazement you *will* "give thanks" because you will realize that this is at once the least and the most you *can* give.

3. "He loved me and gave himself for me"—Baptism, the First Encounter

THAT WE REMEMBER how God loved man is the hallmark of authentic Christian spirituality. But something else is necessary too. It is not enough to remember God's love for mankind as a whole. You must also be deeply aware of that love as it touches *one man* of flesh and blood: you.

Here too you may take your cue from the Apostle to the Gentiles. Paul never tires of reminding Christians of the love of God for mankind, or, as he puts it, of "his great love for man" (Titus 3:4). In defining the object of the divine love Paul over and over again uses the collective: we, us, you—and like a true Southerner occasionally even "you all." Yet he never forgot that it was not mankind but Saul of Tarsus who was knocked to the ground in that encounter with the risen Christ on the road to Damascus. And so he could say, "I have faith in the Son of God who loved me and gave himself for me" (Gal. 2:21). While mindful always of God's "great love for man," Paul realized too that "he loved *me* and gave himself for *me*."

So must you too, Father, constantly adjust your perspective from that magnificent vision of a divine love embracing ALL, to see that same divine love seeking and calling and finding YOU. Yet even here be on guard against "the tyranny of the it." This was not some *thing* which sought out and found you, it was Some One. "It is God himself," said Paul, "who called you to share in the life of his Son, Jesus Christ our Lord; and God keeps faith" (I Cor. 1:9).

Yes, "it is God himself who called you." And when he did, this was the most decisive encounter of your life. It occurred at your baptism. Has it ever bothered you that you and I (perhaps unintentionally but inexorably) have been conditioned away from a full awareness of the magnificence of our baptismal calling? Our seminary training slanted us toward the conviction that our forthcoming ordination was to be *the* climactic event of our lives. And our conditioning ever since has followed the same pattern. Year after year the annual retreat invites us to renew our appreciation of our priestly calling. This is as it should be. It is indeed important that each of us hold fast to a profound reverence for the grace of the priesthood. But I submit to you that this should not be done out of context. It is fine to extol our priestly calling—but not at the cost of saying absolutely nothing about that prior and greater calling of ours: the calling to share God's life and happiness effected at baptism. The climactic event of your life was not when God called you to Holy Orders but when he called you to baptism. That was the first encounter and the decisive one. Nothing more momentous ever happened to you than when all the love behind the Redemption first touched you and brought you personally into vital contact with the God who saves. God effected this contact with you when he came to you at your baptism. Had he not done that, the whole tremendous mystery of God's love for mankind were something which somehow by-passed you. Father, you must never forget that if God had not called you to baptism you might admire his "great love for man" ever so much, but you could not say "he loved *me* and gave himself for *me*."

And has it ever bothered you that we are guilty of pre-empting that grand word "vocation?" We have made it mean exclusively the priestly or religious calling. Any time our Catholic people hear the word "vocation" now, they think instinctively of the priestly or religious vocation. And, of course, in the process they have lost all sense of their *own* vocation, whether to the Christian life or to Christian marriage. In the New Testament the word "vocation" does not mean at all what we have made it mean. In the New Testament the word refers invariably to THE vocation: God's gratuitous call to adoptive sonship issued and effected at baptism. Both we and the Catholic laity are the eventual losers when we tear our vocation to share Christ's priestly powers from its true and larger context of vocation to share Christ.

In this vocation too God was the One who sought and you were the one sought after. "You have not chosen me but I have chosen you" applies to the baptismal vocation also. In this act too the initiative was wholly and exclusively God's. "You are in Christ Jesus by God's act," says St. Paul (I Cor. 1:30). You had no more to do with God's free decision to single you out as the personal object of his love than with his free decision to send his only-begotten Son to redeem and elevate mankind. It pays to remember this too, lest you fall into the trap of taking credit for it yourself, or even of taking *any* of the credit for it yourself. "For who," asks Paul, "singles thee out? And if thou hast received it, why dost thou boast as if thou hadst not received it?" (I Cor. 4:7). I sometimes marvel at our un-witting good fortune in having been baptized in infancy, for when we grow up we have no difficulty at all realizing at least one basic truth about baptism: we personally had absolutely nothing to do with making it happen. And as for any one among us who, as an adult convert, may have made arrangements for his own baptism, I trust he learned well and never forgot the dogma that First Grace can never be merited. The Pelagian temptation to take the credit yourself may be likelier here than in the case of infant baptism, but the simple truth is that every move the adult convert made toward baptism he made under the impulse of grace. Here too it was actually God who made the arrangements. It is equally true here too that "you are in Christ Jesus by God's act."

O that blessed day when God first came to you and first called you! O that blessed day when "his great love for man" ceased being a beautiful abstract poured out on an abstract humanity and became real for YOU. Ever since you can say with St. Paul: "He loved *me* and gave himself for *me*." And you can say it for the same reason: "It is *by the grace of God* that I am what I am."

Father, how often we administer the sacrament of baptism. How routine it becomes. Yet how utterly marvelous it is. What a holy place the baptistry is. God himself is uniquely present there. What God gives there is himself: the Uncreated Grace. His call to his elect is as real and as personal there as it was that night in the bedroom of the boy Samuel. God's own life flows out in created participation there as surely as it did that day in paradise to Adam. (In fact, this is why Christian antiquity always regarded the baptistry as a "second paradise," and why the paradise motif decorates the walls of so many ancient baptistries.) Christ is present there: for this is not at all your act you perform there, it is his act he performs there. The whole mystery of the Redemption and of the Church-as-the-visible-presence-of-Christ is there in the baptistry, made real and existential and effective under sacramental signs and touching this person before you. If only you and I might do there what the bishop at ordination bade us do: "*agnoscite quod agitis,* realize what it is you do." If only what you and I there witness might serve as the backdrop for a meditation on another baptism in another baptistry on another day, when it was not God and *this* child but God and *you*. What thanksgiving such remembering could evoke!

And what a teacher we have in the rite of baptism we perform. This *is* a sacrament and the sacraments *are* signs. By their very nature all signs teach. This is precisely why they are signs. They tell you something. It is only by unique divine intervention that these particular signs called sacraments not only signify or teach, but also effect what they signify. These are very special signs: they not only *tell* you something, they also *do* something. For a long time now we have looked so intently at what they do that we have scarcely taken any notice of what they tell. For roughly the past six-hundred years we have been so preoccupied with the *causality* of the sacraments that we have all but forgotten that they do also teach. We have been so engrossed in them as "effective signs" that we have largely ignored the fact that they are, after all, *signs* and that their purpose is to teach.

What marvelous teaching there is in the sign of baptism! Even today's telescoped and somewhat jumbled version of the ancient rite is a treasurehouse of Christian pedagogy. The Vatican Council's Constitution on the Sacred Liturgy calls for its complete revision, but even so, nothing in our entire liturgy except the Mass is so rich, both in what it teaches and in what it effects.

First of all, the rite teaches, eloquently and repeatedly, that baptism is a personal encounter with God—with the God who here calls and finds someone he loves. Baptism more than anything else is call and response: first call and first response. The rite makes it abundantly clear that baptism is God's call, that this is the DIVINE VOCATION. Have you noticed how you use the words "chosen" and "called" over and over again as you administer baptism? Their obvious intent is to have us see and believe that God is not only present but that he is personally choosing and calling *this* person. Let me quote but a few instances: "We beg you, Lord God, guard this your *chosen one* with the never-failing power of the Cross of Christ with which he has been marked . . . Therefore, accursed devil, depart from this servant of God, for Jesus Christ, our Lord and God, has *called* him to his holy grace and blessing and to the font of baptism . . . Unclean spirit, depart from this creature of God whom our Lord has *called* here to his holy temple in order that he may become a temple of the living God." And then the formal "call," solemnly and dramatically acted out: "John, enter into the temple of God so that you may have part with Christ in everlasting life." "John, come into the Church, that is, into membership in the very body of Christ, so that in and through him you may share everlasting life. John, you have not chosen me; I am choosing you. I hereby call you to share my life so that you may also share my happiness."

This is an authentic ecclesiastical vocation—as personal, as direct, as explicit, as official as the solemn "call" to the priestly vocation in the rite of ordination. The priest-minister issues this call. But this is not just *any* priest who is minister here: he is a priest "with faculties"—he has been officially delegated by the Church to administer this baptism. He acts and speaks in the name of the Church. Actually, not he but the Church issues this call. But the Church is the *"Ur-Sakrament,"* the bodying-forth in visible presence of Christ himself. It was to this Church the Lord said, "he who hears you hears me." When the candidate for baptism hears his name called out at this point it is the voice of the minister, it is the voice of the Church, he *hears*—but this is God who *calls*.

Thus, Father, did God one day call you. *This* is your vocation. And you had nothing to do with it. It was gratuitous. The rite teaches this too: "Almighty and everlasting God, be pleased to look upon this your servant whom *in your goodness* you have called . . ." You had nothing to do with your election. You did not merit it. It was out of his own goodness that God called you. The initiative was wholly God's. "You are in Christ Jesus by God's act" (I Cor. 1:30). ". . . not for any good deeds of our own but because he was merciful, God saved us through the water of rebirth and the renewing power of the Holy Spirit" (Titus 3:5).

There was nothing impersonal about this call: it was unmistakably personal. The rite teaches this too. How else explain the rite's

insistent use of the name? You know, with all our vaunted ingenuity we have yet to devise a designation more personal than a
man's name—and you were called *by name* fourteen times in the
rite of baptism. How apropos God's assurance of long ago: "I am
the Lord, the God of Israel, who calls you by your name" (Isaiah
45:3). And surely it is by more than coincidence that only
those four sacraments which have to do with the Christian vocation
use the name—baptism, confirmation, holy orders and matrimony—
and that the other three do not.

"What's your name, Father?" How often you have been asked
that. But never was so much at stake as when you were asked your
name that day you were baptized. How often you have heard your
name used and called out. But never did it mean more to you than
on that day of your baptism. What did it mean then? Let St. Paul
tell you: "Everything helps to secure the good of those who love
God, those whom he has called in fulfillment of his design. All
those who from the first were known to him he has destined from
the first to be moulded into the image of his Son . . . So predestined,
he called them; so called, he justified them; so justified, he glorified
them (Rom. 8:28-30) . . . The Spirit you have received is not, as
of old, a spirit of slavery to govern you by fear; it is the spirit of
adoption which makes us cry out 'Abba, Father.' The Spirit himself
thus assures our spirit that we are the children of God; and if we are
his children, then we are his heirs too: heirs of God, sharing the
inheritance of Christ" (Rom. 8:15-17).

Remember this, Father. It happened to YOU. Can you then
escape asking often what you ask every Monday at Vespers in the
115th Psalm: "*Quid retribuam Domino pro omnibus quae tribuit
mihi*—What can I repay to the Lord for all that he has given me?"
Yes, how poor you are! *Quid retribuam!* You cannot repay. The
only thing you can do is to *give thanks.* "*Calicem salutis accipiam et
nomen Domini invocabo*—I will take the cup of salvation and call

upon the name of the Lord." You say that you will call upon his
name and praise his goodness. You say that you will give thanks
to God your Saviour at all times and in all places. But if it be the
real thing, your thanksgiving will be more than words only, more
than mere lip service. And so you do not stop when you have said
"Calicem salutis accipiam et nomen Domini invocabo," but you add:
"Vota mea Domino reddam coram omni populo eius—I will keep
my vows to the Lord in the presence of all his people." Yes, if yours
be the *real* thanksgiving, you will fulfill your vows to the Lord.
Baptism is not only a divine call; it is also human response. If it is
true that God called you in baptism, it is equally true that you
answered him. Your answer was not halfhearted or wishy-washy: it
was so firm and positive that you made it in the form of a vow. If
your thanksgiving be the genuine thing, you will fulfill your vows
to the Lord in the presence of all his people. There are vows in
baptism: vows by which you renounced Satan and committed yourself to God, vows by which you turned away from a life of sin and
obligated yourself under contract to live the Christian life of love.

What a powerful and subtle influence words wield over us! The
words and phrases we use affect us deeply—some for better, some
for worse. One which affects us definitely for the worse is that very
favorite Catholic cliché "receiving the sacraments." These apparently harmless words may have done more than we suspect to taint
our whole view of the sacraments with a decidedly non-masculine
passivity. To speak only in terms of *receiving* may result in thinking
not at all of *giving*. Our incessant talk about "receiving the sacraments" has left us with a kind of sponge complex: the bland assumption that all we have to do is to sit back and sop up grace!
(One wonders out loud whether here he may not have at least partial
explanation for the strange but notorious fact that men do not take
so readily to the sacraments as women and children. It is not a
secret that every Sunday looks like "ladies' day" at the Communion
tables of all our parishes. It is of the nature of women and children

to receive. It is of the nature of a mature man to give—and nowhere is this more obvious than in the male sexual role. To achieve fulfillment a real man has got to give; he will feel uncomfortable about and eventually despise any set-up in which he is forever a passive recipient, never a giver—and that includes religion.) All our talk about "receiving the sacraments" obscures one of the great truths of sacramental theology: namely, that every sacrament is not only a sign of *grace* but also a sign of *obligation*. By the very fact one accepts the grace given, he binds himself to live accordingly. Every sacrament is call and response. In every sacrament you enter into a covenant with God by which you contract to live a life that is pleasing to him. This is true of each and all seven of the sacraments. Not only the Eucharist, but each in its own way, is the "new and eternal covenant." As you so well know, this is true of Holy Orders. Be it said to our credit that when we were ordained priests we thought not only of all that we were receiving but we thought also, and very deeply, of all that we were henceforth expected to give. The very fact that you are still wearing that turned-around collar is eloquent testimony that you have not reneged on the contractual obligations you assumed in the sacrament of Holy Orders. What we so easily overlook (and allow the faithful to overlook) is that the contractual obligation assumed at baptism is at least equally pertinent and equally binding.

In fact, not in any of the other sacraments is this idea of reciprocal obligation or response conveyed more clearly than in the rite of baptism. Right at the outset, in the introductory interrogation, this is boldly stated:

Celebrant: What is your name?
Candidate: John.
Celebrant: John, what do you ask of the Church of God?
Candidate: The Faith.
Celebrant: What does the Faith offer you?

Candidate: Everlasting life.

Celebrant: If then it is life you wish to enter, keep the commandments: love the Lord your God with your whole heart and with your whole soul and with your whole mind, and love your neighbor as yourself.

Notice the terms of the contract, the "*quid pro quo*": if you wish to have everlasting life, keep the commandments. *Quid*—what you receive: everlasting life. *Pro quo*—what you must give: love God all the way, love your neighbor.

Like a major theme, the phrase "so that you may have everlasting life" recurs again and again throughout the rite. This is the explicit purpose of both anointings, of the call or vocation into the Church, of the conferral of the baptismal robe and of the lighted candle. What is not always stated but always implied, is that in each and every instance this pledge of everlasting life must be viewed in the contractual context in which it was first introduced: if you want everlasting life, keep the commandments; love God and your neighbor. And lest there be any mistake, you are reminded of this "*quid pro quo*" throughout the rite. To quote at random: "Live from now on in such a way that you may be enabled to be a temple of God . . . Receive this white robe and carry it *unstained* before the judgment seat of our Lord Jesus Christ . . . Receive this lighted candle and keep your baptism above reproach; keep the commandments . . ." If you want to cash in on this pledge of everlasting life, *keep your baptism.*

The full force of this contractual obligation unfolds in the solemn baptismal vows, when by oath you renounced Satan and his works and converted to God the Father, Son and Holy Spirit. That this is indeed an oath is not as clear in our rite today as it was in the early Church. We are told that at this point the candidate for baptism, who was normally an adult rather than an infant, turned to face the

West. In world literature the West has always been associated with darkness, just as the East has been associated with light, because it was thought that the light of day penetrated to the West last. Early Christian tradition had one favored title for Satan: "Prince of Darkness." In their naive way the early Christians assumed that the Prince of Darkness dwelt in the region of darkness. So, if one wanted to look Satan in the eye in face-to-face encounter he turned toward the West. And then with his hand extended in abjuration, in the classical and solemn gesture of oath-making, the candidate for baptism renounced Satan and his works and allurements. The meaning of this particular ritual is exactly the same today even though the sign accompanying it has lost something through the years. But let us not be side-tracked by any sterile comparison between what was and what is. The point is that at *your* baptism *you* took this oath and made this vow. By solemn oath you gave up forever all subservience to Satan and to a life of sin.

But the Christian life is not merely a turning *from*—it is a turning *to*. The Christian life is not essentially the rejection of Satan but the acceptance of God. And so, seconds later at your baptism, you completed this oath by committing yourself to God. As a moment before you had three times repudiated Satan and his kind of life, now you three times profess your conversion to God and his kind of life.

Celebrant:	John, do you believe in God, the Father almighty, Creator of heaven and earth?
Candidate:	I do believe.
Celebrant:	Do you believe in Jesus Christ, his only Son, our Lord, who was born into this world and who suffered?
Candidate:	I do believe.
Celebrant:	Do you believe also in the Holy Spirit. . . ?
Candidate:	I do believe.

Just what was this you did there? More, I assure you, than casually meets the ear. Your key word was "believe." Do you understand what "to believe" really means? I do believe that we don't know what we mean when we say "I do believe." What this implies is not just the giving of your intellectual assent but the giving of yourself. Our modern English word "belief" is a composite of two words: *be* and *lief*. "*Lief*" is the older, obsolete English word for "love." To be-lieve means to be-love: to love completely, all the way, with your whole heart and soul and mind. When you said "I do believe" to God who is Father, Son and Holy Spirit, you gave yourself to him. You made an act of total love. This was your lifetime's most magnificent, most radical conversion. This was the leap—blind, unquestioning. This was your most decisive encounter with God, your all-time yes.

If it is true that in baptism God came to you, it is equally true that you went to God. Your baptism vow is the perfect commentary on that great text in Colossians: "God the Father rescued you from the power of darkness and transferred you into the kingdom of his beloved Son" (Col. 1:13). It was God who rescued and God who transferred. But you responded to both. It was God who acted, but you re-acted. Indeed we agree with Paul that "you are in Christ Jesus *by God's act*"—but you spoke your "yes" to his act. You cooperated *actively* (under the impulse of his grace, to be sure) in both the rescue and the transfer. God encountered you, but you were neither passive nor unresponsive to his presence. You averted from the Evil One and converted to God; you abjured the life of sin and by sworn contract bound yourself to the life of love. Then and there you committed yourself irrevocably to "*thanking* God your Father for making you fit to share the light which saints inherit, for rescuing you from the power of darkness and transferring you into the kingdom of his beloved Son." (Col. 1:12-13).

Most of us were baptized in infancy. Therefore it is imperative that in adult life we deliberately ratify this decisive baptism event.

To doubt that the grace for you to do it is present is to doubt the efficacy of the sacrament—nay it is to doubt the faithfulness of God. The God who called you then calls you now. He has not "withdrawn his face" from you. He does keep faith with you. How significant that when St. Paul said, "It is God himself who called you to share in the life of his Son, Jesus Christ our Lord," he added: "and God keeps faith" (I Cor. 1:9). At first glance that little addition seems irrelevant, out of context. No, it is not. Father, the God who sought you out and called you at your baptism has not changed his mind: he keeps faith. The God who came to you in personal encounter then has not turned aside from you: he keeps faith. He has not recanted the pledge he made to you in that baptism covenant: he keeps faith. What he wants now (as then) is your response, your yes. What he wants to hear now is the fresh ratification of your part of that covenant. Answer him, this God who calls and who keeps faith. Whatever your faithlessness in the past, be not afraid: it *is* the *eternal* covenant; he does keep faith. Renew your solemn abjuration of Satan and his kind of life. Re-commit yourself to that radical conversion you made to God and his kind of life. Say again: "I do believe." To him they are the sweetest words in all this world.

4. "Be converted to me with your whole heart"—Penance, Sacrament of Re-Conversion

THERE IS a remarkable affinity between the sacraments of baptism and penance. One of the Protestant Reformation's bitterest battles raged over this very point. The Reformers did not so much throw out the sacrament of penance as make of it simply the same thing as the sacrament of baptism. They went so far in seeing the affinity between the two that they, in fact, saw no difference between the two. This aberration drew from the Council of Trent the decree that anyone who holds that baptism and penance are one and the same sacrament and not two distinct sacraments is *anathema,* and occasioned the quoting of St. Thomas' famous description of penance as "the second plank of salvation after shipwreck" (Sess. XIV, Can. 2).

We have preserved a questionable reminder of this affinity by coupling baptism and penance under that egregious misnomer "sacraments of the dead." They are alike because both can be validly received when we are supernaturally "dead." But we must admit that we do not find their true and essential "alikeness" here.

True, penance can (and at times does) restore that precious life imparted at baptism. But as we all know, quite often that life has not been lost and does not need to be restored. The real reason why the two are so closely linked is that the sacrament of penance means, in each and every instance, a renewal of baptism. *Commitment* is essential to baptism: *aversio,* the turning from Satan and the sinful life; *conversio,* the turning to God and the Christian life. Penance repeats this, deliberately and dramatically. What you *receive* in the sacrament of penance may or may not be a renewal of what you received at baptism; but in each and every instance what you *give* in the sacrament of penance is a renewal of what you gave at baptism; namely, the conversion effected by your baptismal vows. If the sacrament of penance is not *this* it is nothing. To be a sacrament at all it must be "the sacrament of re-conversion."

Father, I invite you to take a look at the sacrament of penance as we know it and use it in the Church today. One single idea, one single word, bulks very large. The word is: CONFESSION. Have you noticed how we find it all but impossible any more to speak of the sacrament of penance except in terms of "confession?" Our Catholic people never talk about receiving the sacrament of penance —only about "going to confession." Our parish bulletins and pulpit announcements rarely mention the sacrament of penance—almost invariably they tell when "confessions will be heard." We continue to call the place where the sacrament of baptism is given "the baptistry," but we have absolutely no other word for the place where the sacrament of penance is given except "the confessional." Some of our Catholic books and pamphlets now drop all pretense and refer to it simply as "the sacrament of confession." Let's face it: confession has become an obsession with us in the Church today.

What has this done to us? What has been its effect upon us? Auricular confession looms in our minds as *the* important element in the sacrament of penance. Oh, I know, we are careful to teach that contrition is what really counts. And we know well enough that in certain cases auricular confession is not required in administering the sacrament, and hence is not *per se* necessary for validity. All this we teach. *But we must judge our teaching by what our people learn.* Whether or not it be what we intended to teach, our people have learned to make confession their primary concern in their approach to this sacrament. Most of them, in fact, have learned to equate the sacrament with confession. With telling accuracy they regard the whole thing as simply "going to confession." It is this which is the central object of their concern and of their preparation. There is an unmistakable sense that they have "gotten it over with" when the confession itself is finished and behind them. If challenged they might not admit it, but there is a feeling that this is *all* there is to it. The possibility of "bad confessions" worries them ever so much more than the possibility of bad repentance. I am convinced that our overwhelming predilection for the word "confession" tips our hand. It's a dead giveaway. Auricular confession is "it"!

And what has this obsession of ours with confession done to those outside the Church? Father, let me ask you: in your entire pastoral experience has so much as one non-Catholic ever come to you with objections against "the sacrament of penance?" Is it not symtomatic that their objections, invariably, have to do with "confession?" We have pretty well made sure that they do not even know this sacrament by any other name. Whatever it means to Catholics, to our separated brethren it is simply "confession." And because this is so, this great sacrament stands as one of the two or three major barriers between us and them. Because they associate this sacrament exclusively with auricular confession and understand it only in the context of confession, they are repelled by it. Little wonder that they come to us with their tired, worn-out objections: "Confession makes sinning easy . . . This smacks of black magic . . . Confession is not mentioned in the Bible."

And of course they are right. If confession is all there is to it, this sacrament does make sinning easy. If sins are wiped out by auricular confession alone, we do have something magical here. And they are right too about the matter of the Bible: auricular confession, as we understand and practice it in the Church today, is not mentioned in the Bible. And don't quote John 20:23 to them —or to me. This text is helpful but it provides a patent example of reading more into it than is actually there. Auricular confession, as we practice it, is not mentioned in the Bible. But *repentance* is, from cover to cover. One wonders what the general Protestant reaction to this sacrament might be, could we but convince them that repentance is its most essential element so far as the subject is concerned. After all, we still refer to the subject of the sacrament as "the penitent." And this sacrament is unique in that the subject must supply an essential part of the sacramental "sign."

Names *are* important. A rose by any other name might smell as sweet, but naming this sacrament "confession" does not smell as sweet. It has obscured a true appreciation of the sacrament both inside and outside the Church. Should we play the pedant and insist that it be called "the sacrament of penance?" I cannot speak for you, but I do not like that either. The meanings of words shift and change in a living language. To the modern Catholic mind this word "penance" connotes self-denial or is confused with the "three-and-three" Father gives after confession. And it is hard to determine what the word means to the modern Protestant mind.

The Church calls it "*sacramentum poenitentiae.*" Why in heaven's name can't we? Where did we get "penance?" Does anybody know how we ever came to translate the latin word "poenitentia" into the English word "penance?" Did somebody goof way back there and foist a faulty translation off on us which somehow stuck? The English rendering of "*poenitentia*" is "penitence," not "penance." Almost letter for letter it is "penitence." Why not call it "the sacrament of penitence?" But even this leaves something to be desired, because the word "penitence" is falling into disuse and is becoming obsolete in our language. Its synonym is "repentance," and that is the best word. It is current, it is meaningful, it is biblical.

Repentance clearly implies a dual movement of the will: one negative, one positive. It means a turning from and a turning to. It means aversion and conversion. Repentance means both a turning from sin and a turning to love, a turning from Satan and a turning to God. Now the great and radical "repentance" was baptism. It was in baptism that this turning or commitment was first made. In the Easter Vigil and at other solemn landmarks in the Christian life we encourage our Catholic people to renew their baptism vows—vows which are so explicitly both aversion and conversion. But let us also recognize that the Lord has given us a *sacrament* in which the baptism vows are, at least implicitly, to be renewed. The close affinity between the sacraments of baptism and penance lies precisely in this: penance renews baptism. There is no true sacrament of penance without repentance. And repentance is simply a renewal of baptism's commitment: aversion and conversion.

Take careful note that it is "*Sacramentum* Poenitentiae." There is question here not merely of repentance, but of the *sacrament* of repentance. We deal here with the *outward sign* of repentance. All acts of the penitent are geared to the signifying or "sign-izing" of repentance.

This is important because this is the context in which we must view all the acts of the penitent—auricular confession included. The importance and true relevance of confession lies in its relationship to repentance, in its ability to "sign-ize" repentance. The eminent Dutch theologian, Bernard Häring, says: "The interior disposition of contrition (repentance) is manifested externally by confession and elevated to the sacramental efficacy of sign" (*Law of Christ* (Baltimore: Newman), 1961, I, p. 450). This is the purpose or relevance of auricular confession: to serve as *an external sign of repentance*. We confess our sins in order to show our repentance in external sign. And *what* a sign it can at times be! Is there a man

among us who has not been moved to quiet tears by it? How sheep-
ishly grateful we are at such times for the screen and for the
impregnable privacy of the box! Love is not the noblest human act.
Repentance is. Repentance is love, once dead, now risen and living
anew. To witness this miracle of grace can be almost unbearably
touching as each of us can attest.

Jesus of Nazareth found it so too: he could not resist its power
to move. He reserved the most beautiful of all his parables, the
Prodigal Son, as his medium for presenting the theme of repentance.
It was because of her repentance that he immortalized Mary
Magdalen: "I promise you, in whatever part of the world this gospel
is preached, the story of what she has done shall be told . . . to
preserve her memory" (Mark 14:9). How highly he prized repentance! He assured us that even in heaven it rates first place: "So it
is, I tell you, in heaven; there will be more rejoicing over one
sinner who repents than over ninety-nine souls that are justified
and have no need of repentance" (Luke 15:7). It was repentance
which made the difference between Judas and Peter. You and I,
Father, are privileged to witness repentance every time we "hear
confessions." How much more meaningful sacramental confession
could be to our Catholic people, could we but get them to see it
not merely as an anxious enumeration of their sins but as the sign
par excellence of their re-conversion.

Repentance is also the context of the Act of Contrition. It is its
complete and only context. The Act of Contrition is simply sign-
making. It is our way of putting repentance into an external,
perceptible sign—the most common sign in all the world: words.
This is its only purpose. If the Act of Contrition be not this, it is
nothing.

Because it includes contrition the sacrament of penance should be
a profound "religious experience" for each of us every time. How
we Catholics shy away from the phrase. "Religious experience"
conjures up images of tent revivals and shouting evangelism. It is

not for us. We are somehow above all that. In fact we consider it
rather bad form to betray the slightest emotion in our practice of
religion. Yet the very word we use here means exactly that. "Contrition" is a word we have borrowed from the latin "*conterere-con-
tritum*"—to be crushed to pieces, to be torn to shreds! Even the staid
Council of Trent spoke of "the *feeling* of contrition" (Sess. XIV,
Cap. 4).

While we are at it, let us pause for a steady look at the "Act of
Contrition." It is a flawless expression of repentance. It is, in fact,
just a little too flawless. It is a precise theological formula—but is
it prayer? To recite the Act of Contrition is to get the distinct feeling
that a theologian is looking over your shoulder checking off all the
essential elements of repentance. Prayer is converse with God—
with the God who is our Father. The prayer of repentance is
the returning prodigal's artless stammering to the Father who
has run to meet him and who falls upon his neck and smothers
him with kisses. The "Act of Contrition" does not ring very true.
How many of us talk like this? Polished, precise, ever so correct,
ever so artificial. Why must we take this stance when we talk to
God our Father? Probably because it is the only one we know. We
learned the "Act of Contrition." 'Way back when, we memorized
it—agonizingly. We have not varied one jot or tittle of it since—
and we dare not.

This is true of practically all our prayers. Almost all of them are
"canned prayers." We learned them by rote from parent or teacher,
or we read them out of a book. All our lives we Catholics have
been spoon-fed our prayers. They are, of course, not *our* prayers at
all. They are somebody else's. The sad truth is that we Catholics,
priests included, cannot pray. All we can do is *recite*—sometimes
with meaning and advertence, quite often with neither. How revealing that we usually talk about "*saying* our prayers" rather than
just "praying." Have you ever noticed how lost our Catholic people
are without a "prayer book" or the familiar, memorized prayer-

formulas? And we priests come unglued when faced with the prospect of "composing" a prayer. We have never done it and we frankly do not know how. Go to a banquet or public function: the Jewish rabbi or Protestant minister gets up for the invocation and what he says may not be so good but it is *his*—and at times it is very good. Now and then I have heard one of these men get up before a banquet or a convention and pray: simply, in his own words, in a way that lifts up the mind and stirs the heart. One of us gets up, and what does he say? "Bless us, O Lord, and these thy gifts . . ." And when we pray publicly with the faithful, whether our prayer be for peace or for priestly vocations or for a deceased parishioner or for whatsoever, it is usually three Hail Mary's—not one but three. The good old Hail Mary! It fits every need and purpose and occasion—or at least we make it fit. It is simply not in us (or in our people) to *talk* to God—freely, from the heart, like sons who cry out "Abba, Father." It is almost impossible for us just to talk to him; somehow we feel that we have to make a nice speech to him.

And this is the inevitable way in which we talk to our Father to tell him that we are crushed by our sins and that we want to love him: we make a speech, we *recite* the "Act of Contrition." Father, let's face it: that dear old "Act of Contrition" can be a positive hindrance to real repentance. It is second-nature with us now. It occasions neither effort nor thought and it rolls so easily off the tongue. It may well have become a meaningless cliché. What is so sacrosanct about it? Why have we made it a sacred cow in the sacrament of penance? Why do some of us insist that it be said without fail before we give absolution? The plain truth is that the "Act of Contrition" which we have canonized is not necessary to the *sacramentum poenitentiae.* But one thing is absolutely necessary: real repentance.

Please do not interpret this as a one-man campaign to rub out the "Act of Contrition." If it does what it purports to do, keep it; if it is what it is supposed to be, well and good. But I do not hesitate to say that wherever it has become a handy stereotype which has degenerated into a hindrance rather than a help to the external expression of *true* repentance, throw it out! Far better that a man express his repentance in halting, inadequate, untheological words that come from his heart, than that he rattle off a precise theological formula which comes neither from the heart nor from the head. Occasionally I advise penitents after confession to forget about reciting the "Act of Contrition," and tell them I want to hear them talk to God in their own way to assure him that they have turned from their sins and turned to him. After the initial shock, they do. What I hear is real prayer, magnificent prayer. At times I am downright embarrassed: feeling like an eavesdropper who hears awkward intimacies lovers whisper to one another which no third party should hear. I challenge you to cite me a better prayer of repentance than that of the Publican who stood in the rear of the temple, bowed his head and murmured "O God, be merciful to me the sinner." Theologically, as an act of perfect contrition, that leaves much to be desired. But do you remember what the Lord said about it? "This man, I tell you, went home justified rather than the other" (Luke 18:13–14).

Father, the *sacramentum poenitentiae* has a double relevance in your life: as a man and as a priest.

As a man you need it. In her Code of Canon Law the Church tells you that you need it "frequently" (Canon 125). She knows—she is your Mother. You are indeed *God's* man. But you are withal a man: cut from the same cloth as your weak brethren who go to their knees before you and with such shattering forthrightness say to you: "Bless me, Father; I have sinned . . ." Like them, you too mean only to love. But like them you fall. You need repentance. Certainly you need it *now*. Of two things I am sure. First, the grace of repentance *is* available to you *now*. It is yours for the taking. Secondly, I am sure that some of you have not taken the grace of sacramental repentance for some time. To you, whoever you are, I address myself. Make no mistake about it, Father: in your heart of hearts you want very much to love God. You *do* seek him. Love is noble indeed. But repentance is nobler still. Repentance is love, once dead, risen and living anew. The God you seek calls to you now. The God you seek is the God who seeks you. *"Hodie si vocem eius audieritis, nolite obdurare corda vestra*—Today if you should hear his voice, do not harden your hearts" (Psalm 94). Yes, that's all: *nolite obdurare corda vestra.* Taking or rejecting the grace of repentance was the only difference between Peter and Judas!

As a man you *need* the sacrament of repentance, as a priest you *give* it. How splendid your mediatorship here: reconciling errant sons with a loving Father! In the secrecy of the box, again and again, you witness first-hand this touching return, this magnificent conversion. What an exalted grace this is! You the peacemaker between Father and adopted child. You the dispenser of God's pardon. What a privilege—and what a responsibility! How wonderfully you meet it *inside* the sacrament, in the act of dispensing God's pardon. But what about outside?

True, you actually dispense God's pardon only in the sacramental act. But you are a marked man. Wherever you go, whatever you do, whatever you say, you are known as the man who dispenses God's pardon. You, more than any man in all this world, must be kind to sinners—always and everywhere. You, more than any man in all this world, must hate the sin but love the sinner—always and everywhere. You must despise gluttony, but you must never give the impression that you despise the alcoholic; you must abhor sins of impurity, but you may never abhor the adulterer or the mastur-bator or the homosexual; you must hate sins of injustice, but you dare not hate the racial bigot or the employer who pays unjust wages; you must detest heresy, but you may never detest the heretic. You are the dispenser of God's pardon, and therefore yours must be the true priestly heart which is big enough and generous enough to embrace and welcome all of sinful, suffering humanity. Nothing so becomes the priest as compassion. Thank God, we have it in the confessional. But do we always have it outside? I am convinced that most of the harm we do as confessors we do outside the confessional.

Whether we realize it or not, we dispensers of God's pardon can cause irreparable harm by an unguarded remark or a careless jest, even in ordinary conversation. We just never know who is listening. We never know what unhappy, groping sinner is destroyed by what we say or even by the way we say what we say. One careless, loud-mouthed priest can so easily give the impression at least to some one that all priests are hard and cynical. It is so ridiculously easy for any one of us to give the impression that priests despise not only the sin but also the sinner—and for some poor struggling sinner within earshot the last thread is cut, the door is slammed shut forever. We have got to be eternally aware, not only inside the sacrament of penance but outside, that it is not our pardon we dispense but God's. If God's mercy be above all his works, we must never be guilty of placing it in jeopardy because it is through us God has chosen to pour it out upon the people he loves and means to have for his very own. Look you to it!

5. "The just man lives by faith"— Priestly Faith

FAITH! How significant that this was the first request you ever made of God. Faith was what you were after when you made your first response to his first call at baptism. Do you remember how your baptism began? "What do you ask of the Church of God?" "Faith." You began your life with God by asking for faith. And rightly so, for "the just man lives by faith" (Rom 1:17) ". . . without faith it is impossible to please God" (Heb. 11:6). This precious indispensable may in the meantime have gotten a bit wobbly and tattered, but what counts is that you have it. And don't you ever forget that, whatever you may have had to do with *keeping* it, you had absolutely nothing to do with *getting* it. You would not now have faith nor could you ever have gotten it if God had not made the first move. We must not let our use of the cliché, "gift of faith," blind us to the simple fact that it *is* a gift. The faith you have, Father, is a pure gift from God. He gave it to you at your baptism. It was then you asked for it and it was then you got it. You cannot repay it. All you can do is "give thanks" for it.

Father, what do you make of faith? This is a fair question, because the odds are that you make rather less of it than it is. This neo-Scholastic age of ours has come to regard faith as relating exclusively to the intellect. The textbooks you and I used in the seminary belabored the point that faith is an act of the "intellect assenting." Faith, we were told, is an act of the mind. Of course it is that—but it is by no means only that. Intellectual assent is not what the Bible means by "faith." There it connotes a commitment involving the *whole* man, not just his mind. Péguy was so right to have reminded us that "the heart too has its reasons for believing." And Bruce Vawter writes: "What engages man's faith is not what engages his mind only . . . Man is more apt to believe 'in his bones' as we say, or 'in his heart of hearts.' The absolute and irrevocable commitment that is expressed in martyrdom we do not think of primarily as an intellectual act . . . We think of it, and the martyr thinks of it, as an act of faith performed by his whole being." (*Worship*, Sept., 1960) Faith is an engagement of the whole man, not just of his intellect. Faith is the act of an "I," not just of a brain or an "it."

As we noted previously, in the English language we have a synonym for the word "faith" which is "belief." We make this word by putting together two shorter words: "be" and "lief." "Lief" is quite obsolete in our language now, but it is the older form of our current word "love." To be-lieve means, really, to be-love: to love completely, to give or commit yourself without reserve. In your baptism you were asked three times whether you believed in God: Father, Son and Holy Spirit. Each time you answered solemnly: "I do believe—I do be-love God; He is my be-loved; I love him completely, with the love of my whole mind and soul and strength; I commit myself without reserve to the Father, to the Son and to the Holy Spirit." It was precisely here you were given faith, precisely here you made the definitive act of faith. This was more than your intellect saying yes to certain truths about God. This was YOU saying yes to GOD!

Apropos of this, have you ever noticed the unorthodox grammar of the Creed? Ordinarily the latin verb 'credere' takes the dative case. But the Creed does not say *"Credo Deo Patri . . . Filio . . . Spiritui Sancto."* It says *"Credo in Deum Patrem . . . in Filium . . . in Spiritum Sanctum."* In an effort to avoid sounding too off-beat altogether, our English translation pussyfoots a little and makes a compromise with this exceptional grammatical form. "I believe *in* God the Father" is not the correct translation of *"Credo in Deum Patrem."* The Creed does not have *"in Deo Patre";* it has *"in Deum Patrem."* This is the *active* "in"; it is the "in" of motion which takes the accusative case. The translation, to be quite precise, should go: "I believe INTO God the Father . . . INTO Jesus Christ . . . INTO the Holy Spirit." Faith is much more than an act of your intellect assenting to the truth of Three Persons in one God: it is an ENTERING INTO, an encounter, a commitment of *yourself.*

Incidentally, you get the truer dimension of faith from the use to which you put the word in Christian marriage. The words "keeping true faith" and "fidelity" occur several times in our rite of matrimony. "Accept this ring as a pledge of my fidelity—as my pledge that I will keep the faith." What a personal commitment the word *"fides"* or "faith" means here! The young man who makes *this* act of faith is not merely assenting intellectually to certain truths about marriage. He is handing over *himself* to his bride and to his unborn children, all of himself: heart, mind, skills, strength, body, affections. Don't tell him that *fides* or *fidelitas* involves just his intellect—he knows what it means! And you see here something else about faith we today often forget: *at its deepest level faith does not have to do with truths or doctrines or things but with persons.* Faith commits you not to some*thing* but to some*one!* The "faith" of Christian marriage shows you that faith is not an "it" called intellectual assent but an "I," and also that faith is not relation with an "it" called truth but surrender to a "thou." Faith, at its deepest point, is not "it-it" but "I-Thou."

Father, if this be true of ordinary Christian Faith, how much more of yours! Your commitment-by-faith is so much more definitive and clean-cut than the layman's. You have literally staked everything on your surrender to God. Your acceptance of the priestly vocation is a tremendous act of faith seen in this fuller dimension. Your whole life as a priest is living witness to *this* kind of faith. This faith by which you accepted the priesthood involved not just intellectual assent: it meant a commitment of your heart, of your loins, of your normal human drives and affections, of your pocketbook, of your will, of ALL of you. We have all laughed at the banter heard occasionally in exclusively clerical gatherings, to the effect that we priests have "had it" if all this isn't so. We laugh along—but what heavenly wisdom in this earthy statement! What abundant faith is implied in our priestly vocation!

And in the light of this deeper view of faith do not most so-called "problems of faith" find their solution? A worried parishioner kneels before you to confess "doubts in certain matters of faith." Don't you hear the solution shouted out at you by the very fact that this man is even now making the great act of faith by baring his soul to you and submitting to the power of the keys? This man's faith is what he IS and what he DOES; it is not the inevitable misgivings which bob up to trouble any alert mind. I think it was Bruce Marshall who said "Doubt is an implicate of faith. Faith does not mean the absence of doubt. It means giving God the benefit of the doubt about the doubt." And I am sure it was he who took the well-known quote from St. James and turned it into: "Faith without *doubts* is dead." Theologians may quibble about his license with the word "doubt," but no one can cavil at the wisdom of what he says. To inquire, to call into question, is the normal and natural business of the human mind. A query or misgiving hatched in the intellect-as-such does not even touch faith. It is the *will* which has the last word in faith; it is *you*. What a busy, unsupervised intellect happens to pump up into consciousness does not trespass upon the precincts of faith at all. If anything, these musings form the backdrop of a true act of faith: a deliberate renewal of your commitment despite the misgivings.

There is a built-in paradox to Christian faith. It is indeed private and deeply personal: it is I-Thou between each individual and God. But at the same time it is not "private" at all: it is fundamentally social or corporate. *The way you got it* tells you this. God gave you the supernatural virtue of faith at baptism as a concomitant of First Grace. The nature of supernatural faith is tied-in to the nature of supernatural life. Now you got the supernatural life by incorporation into a *community,* into Christ's body the Church. It is Christ's risen body which lives by this divine life we call Grace. You came to have it in the first place by being made a living member of that Body, by sharing the life of the mother organism. And this is the way you continue to have it. God gives you his life not directly but indirectly, not privately or individually but corporately. And since faith is a concomitant of First Grace, it too is essentially social or communitarian. ". . . regard not my sins but the faith of thy Church."

This is a truth heavy with consequence in the spiritual life. You do not have faith either *by* yourself or *for* yourself. Faith is not private but social.

Most especially, Father, is this true of *your* faith. You received not only the sacrament of baptism but the sacrament of holy orders as well. Holy orders and matrimony, in a way that is unique, are "social" sacraments. (Of course *all* the sacraments are social or ecclesial, but I think there is validity in holding that these two are that in a way all their own.) The sacrament of Holy Orders gave a special modality to sanctifying grace in you, and consequently a special modality to the infused virtue of faith which was and is its adjunct. Since your ordination, Father, sanctifying grace is not quite the same in you as in the layman. Therefore the virtue of faith is not quite the same in you as in the layman. In *you,* faith bears a *specifically social* orientation. *You,* Father, do not merely *have* the faith: God has singled you out as his primary means of *giving* it. Because you are a priest you *have* the faith and you *keep* the faith only by *giving* the faith!

This is obvious in the fact that as a priest you administer the sacraments. You are thus the dispenser of Grace and, concomitantly, the dispenser of faith. They *are* the "sacraments of faith."

But this is true also in a deeper and less obvious sense. Faith in men is sustained by *actual* grace. Now the priest is the world's foremost "actual grace." Cardinal Suhard coined the arresting adage: the priest is a sacrament. By this he means that the priest is an external sign used by God to cause internal actual grace. God causes grace and increases faith in men *not only* by the signs of water and chrism and imposition of hands: he also causes grace and strengthens faith in them by the external sign of a weak and bumbling flesh-and-blood man clad in priestly garb!

You must be deeply aware, therefore, that as a priest you communicate faith to men not only by administering the sacraments, but also by the *manner* in which you administer the sacraments— especially by the manner in which you administer the sacrament of the Eucharist, by the manner in which you celebrate Holy Mass. The personal experience of everyone of us confirms this. Perhaps you know the story of the eleven-year-old boy serving Mass in his native Corsica: having observed how faithlessly the priest that morning celebrated Mass, coming home and saying in disgust: "*He* doesn't believe in it, why should I?" The boy's name was Napoleon Bonaparte. When we celebrate Mass, Father, these impressionable young sons of the Church do not only *serve* us, they also *observe* us. And so do the people, whom the Mass calls "God's holy people." Assembled here for this "*mysterium fidei*" from the midst of a savagely faithless world, they cry out for confirmation of their faith. It is to God they cry, but it is to us they look! What do they see, Father? Whether we realize it or not (but somehow realize it we must), they lean on us as the living proof of their holy Catholic Faith. In their need they look to us as unfailing towers of strength, neither realizing nor understanding that, like the first Apostles, we too can be men of little faith. Whether we like it or not, we are signs of faith for them: signs confirming their faith—or signs destroying it.

As a priest it is also your office to communicate faith to men through "the ministry of preaching." Without prejudice to the efficacy of the sacraments, Holy Writ says flatly: "Faith comes by hearing" (Rom. 10:17).

Father, do you subscribe to that? To judge by appearances, many of us do not. It is positively amazing how so many of us ignore the primacy of preaching in our priestly ministry. Our attitude, implied if not explicit, is that preaching is sort of an "and also" in our priestly office but not of its essence. This is astounding and totally unwarranted. The example and words of the Lord, the example and counsel of the Apostles, the witness of the sacred liturgy: all cry out in massive refutation. "Faith comes by hearing"—*now* as then.

Jesus cast himself not in the role of organizational genius or master builder or even of wonder worker. He spent his public ministry *preaching*. You have his own word for it that this was, in fact, its purpose: "Let us go into the next country towns so that I can preach there too; *it is for this that I have come*" (Mark 1:38). He allotted three hours to offering his redemptive sacrifice; he devoted the better part of three years to preaching. The gospels do not even record his actual institution of most of the sacraments, but page after page they are filled with what he preached. We have *faith* that he personally instituted seven sacraments in the Church; we have *proof* that he personally instituted preaching in the Church: "Go into the whole world and preach the gospel to every creature; he who believes (upon hearing your preaching) and is baptized shall be saved" (Mark 16:16). And in his last prayer the night before he died he said: "Father . . . not only for these do I pray, but for all those who *through their word* are to believe in me" (John 17:20).

Notice too that the absolute inviolability of the office of preaching was one of the reasons for the institution of the diaconate in the infant Church. "Come then, brethren, you must find seven men . . . while we devote ourselves to prayer and to the *ministry of preaching*" (Acts 6:4).

And St. Paul! Paul the organization man, the busy founder, trusted spiritual director, baptizing, confirming, ordaining. Yes, but above all, first and foremost, Paul the PREACHER. With Paul preaching came first. In First Corinthians he wrote: "Christ certainly did not send me to baptize but to preach. . . . Woe betide me if I do not go on preaching the gospel." And his advice to the priest Timothy was: "Preach the word, in season and out of season" (II Tim. 4:2).

And the liturgy! So often we priests appeal to the importance and efficacy of the Mass as a kind of back-handed excuse for our indifference to preaching. "After all, it's the Mass that counts . . . Sure, the Protestants work harder at their preaching, but then that's all they have . . ." And so forth and so on. Out of our own mouths we are condemned! From the very earliest times the Church has integrated preaching with the Mass. To underscore their inseparability, the liturgy from the beginning combined into one "the liturgy of the Word" and "the liturgy of the Bread." The Constitution on the Sacred Liturgy says that both of them "form but one single act of worship" (Par. 56).

The homily or sermon has been part of the Mass from Apostolic times. For Sunday Mass it is *de praecepto,* for weekday Mass it is warmly encouraged. If you are indifferent about the Sunday *sermon,* then you are indifferent about Sunday *Mass.* Not to prepare for the sermon is not to prepare for Mass. It is as much a part of your ministry to give the faithful the Word of God in your preaching as it is to give them the Word of God in Holy Communion! The "bread of life" which you break at Mass includes not only the *fractio panis* but also the sermon. "God's word," Augustine dared say, "is no less important than the Body of Christ." And St. Gregory the Great beautifully compares preaching to parenthood: "He who is the brother of Christ by believing, becomes his mother by preaching. Indeed (the preacher) *begets* the Lord whom he has infused into the heart of his hearer; and he becomes mother by his preaching if, through what he says, the love of God is begotten in the soul of his neighbor" (*Hom. III in Evang.*).

Grinding out a sermon Sunday after Sunday, whether you have the touch or not, becomes such a burden. It developes into almost hypnotic routine. Enthusiasm (whether in the sense of God-filledness or even in the accepted sense) is pretty hard to come by. But somehow you and I have got to realize, Father, that it is when we stand there before God's holy people hungry for the bread of life and open our mouths to preach, we are taking up the FIRST duty of our priestly calling. Your bishop shares in the priesthood of the Apostles and you share in it through him. Well, when the Apostles were *sent* they were sent TO PREACH. "I do not count my life precious compared with my work," said the Apostle Paul. Then he went on to say what this work, more precious than life, was: ". . . my work, which is to finish the course I run: the task of *preaching* which the Lord Jesus has given me, in proclaiming the good news of God's grace" (Acts 20:24). Father, this is *your* work too. When you, God's man, turn around toward your people on Sunday to preach, you are then and there stepping into your most proper role, you are taking up your first and most sacred duty. We never forget that going in to the *altar* of God to offer sacrifice is our noblest duty, but we do tend to forget that going in to the *pulpit* of God to preach the word is our *first* duty. How truly right and fitting that both should be integrated into "the one single act of worship," the Mass. To begin *Mass* without preparation is not fitting, but to begin *preaching* without preparation is a sin! There is a story told of the great Lacordaire receiving two seminarians who came to him shortly before their ordination to ask this master for some helpful hints on preaching. "I have only two things to say to you about preaching," he replied. "One, never preach without preparation. Two, if ever you do, remember that it is matter for your next confession."

And lest you think Saul of Tarsus or Lacordaire dated, Pope John XXIII wrote in "The Priestly Life" on March 13, 1959: "In the Missal are the Two Testaments. Preaching these to the people is the *principal work* and the *high point* of the Catholic Priesthood."

Finally, remember how solicitously the Church impressed upon you the importance of your ministry of preaching on that memorable day when she made you a priest. In the bishop's solemn charge to you before ordination, when he said *"Sacerdotem oportet offere,"* in the same breath he added *"et praedicare."* The office *proper* to you as a priest is to offer sacrifice *and* to preach. His parting plea to you in that instruction was: "Let your teaching be a spiritual medicine for the people of God . . . May you thus build up, by your example and by your preaching, the house, that is the family of God."

And so do you *now*, O priest of God, "stir up the grace of God that is in thee." Stir up the grace of baptism which included faith. Rededicate yourself to the total personal commitment this faith implies. And stir up the unique faith that is in thee by the imposition of hands of the priesthood: that faith you can hold onto only by passing on to others. Never forget that it is through you God has chosen to give the faith to his people: by means of the sacraments of faith you administer, by means of the witness of your priestly life, by means of the ministry of your preaching. Yours is an immense honor. A most sacred trust. Look you to it. Believe *into* it. Re-commit yourself. "Stir up the grace of God that is in thee by the imposition of hands" (II Tim. 1:6).

6. "Faith comes by hearing"—
Reading and Preaching God's Word

"FIDES EX AUDITU"! Sacred Scripture offers few statements less ambiguous than this. Yes, faith comes by hearing—but not unless you and I have faith that it does. You and I have got to restore the preaching of God's word to its central place in our priestly ministry. We have got to see that Pope John XXIII knew what he meant and meant what he said: ". . . preaching is the principal work and the high point of the Catholic priesthood." One of the great speeches thus far in Vatican Council II was the talk by Cardinal Ritter of St. Louis on October 4, 1963, in which he warned the Council Fathers that all their efforts to renew the Church are doomed to failure unless the ministry of preaching, in eclipse with us since Trent, be again restored to its primary place. It is not hyperbole to say that the Church succeeds or fails in her mission in exact ratio to how well or how poorly she preaches the word of God to the people of God. It is you and I whom the Church has sent to do her preaching. If we do not preach well the Church does not preach well.

The attitude toward preaching presents a real paradox in the Church today: nothing interests the people more, few things interest the priest less. You need not be a sociologist to know that what the people want more than any other one thing from their priest is good preaching. Even though they may not be conscious of it, they sense instinctively that faith does indeed come by hearing—*their* faith. The kind of preaching that stirs their faith is the one thing they want most from us, because somehow they realize (even if we do not) that this is the one thing they *need* most from us.

But we do not take our ministry of preaching especially seriously. None of us would deny its importance, but few of us would give it first place. Most of us regard it as a necessary kind of "and also" in our over-all ministry. Could any of us say that what attracted us to the priesthood was the sacred office of preaching God's word? "Vocation Directors," of both the diocesan and religious brand, are hard at work throughout our country appealing to the ideals of our Catholic youth. But how many are looking for promising preachers, or how often do they propose the office of preaching as the reason to "come follow him?"

We are, of course, well protected in our nonchalance toward preaching. It is to "captive audiences" we do our preaching. Because they are there they have to listen, whether the sermon that particular Sunday happens to be good, bad or indifferent. Rarely do we disturb ourselves by wondering how many others are *not* there precisely because the preaching is not so good. And of course our jobs do not depend on how well we preach. Perhaps one of the main reasons for the amazing vitality of Protestantism is the better quality of Protestant preaching. And surely one of the reasons why it *is* better is that the Protestant minister knows his job depends on how effectively he preaches the word of God. I have never heard of one of our pastors being removed from office because he was not very serious about his preaching.

We priests recognize and accept our commission to administer the sacraments to our people. We are admirably conscientious about our pastoral duty in this regard. But we do not bring quite the same sensitive pastoral concern to our commission to preach the word to the people. Why? Our commission to preach to our people is as authentic and as explicit as our commission to give them the sacraments. How long since you read the pagella of "faculties" from your Bishop? You should try it—it makes very interesting reading. For one thing, you will note that the power and commission to preach shares equal billing with the power and commission to celebrate Mass, to baptize, to absolve. I do not know about yours, but my list of diocesan "faculties" puts preaching before all the others. The pagella from my Archbishop lists eighteen separate faculties: the commission to baptize is number two, to celebrate Holy Mass is number five, to give absolution in the sacrament of penance is number thirteen. But *number one* reads thus: *"Praedicandi Verbum Dei in ecclesiis et oratoriis*—Preaching the Word of God in the churches and oratories (of the Archdiocese)." Surely it is not just by accident that the pastoral commission to preach the word takes precedence over everything else. It is placed first because it holds first place. "Preaching is the principal work and the high point of the Catholic priesthood." In fact, it was not always given us. There were times in the history of the Church when preaching was restricted to bishops. This was regarded as such a sacred and important function of the Apostolic office that it could not be shared even with the presbyterate. Celebrating Mass, yes. But preaching, no!

The sacraments were instituted by the Lord, and for that reason we who administer them have tremendous faith in their power and efficacy. I wonder then why we ministers of the word do not have equal faith in the power and efficacy of our preaching because that too, no less than the sacraments, was instituted by the Lord. Because of their divine origin we believe that Christ himself acts in the sacraments. I wonder why we do not believe equally strongly and for the very same reason that Christ himself acts in the "sacrament of preaching." The Apostles were deeply aware that their preaching was the very word *of* God and not merely words *about* God. Thus Paul could say to the Thessalonians: "We thank God for this, that when you received the word of God which you heard from us, you accepted it not as the word of men but as what it really is: the word of God which is at work in you believers" (I Thess. 2:13).

We too must approach our office of preaching with the deep awareness that the word we preach is none other than the effective, saving word of God. Through your lips and mine he sends it out into the minds and hearts of "the people he means to have for his very own." He guarantees that it will not return empty, for thus says the Lord God: "Just as from the heavens the rain and snow come down and do not return there till they have watered the earth, making it fertile and fruitful, giving seed to him who sows and bread to him who eats, so shall my word be that goes forth from my mouth: it shall not return to me empty but shall do my will, achieving the end for which I sent it" (Isaias 55:10–11). As he promised, the risen Christ sends out the Holy Spirit; and he fulfils that promise when we get up to preach, for it is in our preaching he sends him out. What the Lord said on the first Easter Sunday he never ceases to say to his Church: "receive you the Holy Spirit." We must be aware that the ordinary, divinely-instiuted means by which this redeemed people receives the Spirit is your preaching and mine. Our preaching is no mere passing-on of information: it is Spirit-laden and creative, it elicits a response, it stirs faith. As God's prophets, you and I communicate the word of God. It is by our preaching that we do it, and our doing of it becomes that sacramental action by which the God for whom we speak turns towards men and addresses them, calls them, invites them to faith, to yes-saying, to commitment. *Agnoscite quod agitis!*

If faith comes by hearing the word of God's man, it certainly comes also by hearing the word of God. Sacred Scripture is the word of God. God encourages his people to read his word, but above all he means for them to *hear* his word. This is one of the principal reasons why he calls them together on the Lord's day to form a church or *ecclesia*. They assemble in order to hear God's word. More and more we are coming to see that the faithful assemble on Sunday to join actively in the communal offering of the Eucharist. But we must also see that there is another major purpose in forming this assembly: to join actively in the communal hearing of the word of God. Who is to say that the "liturgy of the word" is any less important than the "liturgy of the bread and cup?" The Vatican Council's Constitution on the Sacred Liturgy refuses to admit any such subordination and says pointedly that the two form but one single act of worship (Cfr. par. 56).

St. Augustine was quite to the point: "The Word of God is no less important than the Body of Christ." The two belong together. It was so from the beginning. The first "church" in salvation history, the first liturgical assembly of God's people (*qehal Yahweh*), took place during the exodus at the foot of Mount Sinai. This assembly first listened to God's word, and only after that joined in the sacrifice. In the twenty-fourth chapter of Exodus we read that Moses, on returning from the top of the mountain to the assembly at its base, ". . . took the Book of the Covenant and read it aloud to the people, who answered: 'All that the Lord has said we will heed and do.' Then he took the blood (of the young bulls offered as holocausts) and sprinkled it on the people saying: 'This is the blood of the covenant which the Lord has made with you in accordance with all these words of his.' " Father, this same God has made a new covenant with a new people of God—not in the blood of goats and calves but in the blood of his own Son (Hebrews 9:19). As Moses did, so do we. At Sunday Mass, before this new people of God renews this covenant in the blood of that Son, we first take the Book of the

New Covenant and read it aloud to them so that they too can
make the response: "All that the Lord has said we will heed
and do."

The Bible is "the Church's book," and no one has ever doubted
that it must therefore be the priest's book too. But it must be
that today, perhaps more than ever before. Never has it been
more imperative that the priest take up the Bible. "*Tolle et lege*"
has never been more relevant than it is today.

I say this for two reasons. First, we are unquestionably at a
point in the Church's history where she has "re-discovered" the
Bible. This is not to imply that the Church, at any point in her
history, stopped using the Bible. But there is something particularly massive and pentecostal about the return to the Scriptures
throughout the Church today. The "biblical movement" is not
just a slogan, it is a reality. More and more we are directed back
to the Scriptures in the development of our theology and in the
content of our preaching. There is a growing suspicion that neither
St. Thomas nor even the Council of Trent yield the full and
final deposit of the holy Catholic Faith. More and more we are
returning to Sacred Scripture to discover the true and pure face
of the Church.

Our scripture scholars are pressing ahead at a dazzling clip. The
poor parish priest whose seminary scripture course dates back
twenty, ten or even five years is not merely impressed—he is quite
likely dismayed and confused and scared to open his mouth about
the Bible or about anything in it. In a kind of frantic effort to
keep somewhat abreast he probably buys a few books and sub-
scribes to a few periodicals on the "new look" in scripture studies.
But even more probably he watches his time go down the drain
in the chaotic demands of his daily ministry and never quite
gets around to cracking those fine books and ends up growing
only more insecure about the whole thing. Well, Father, something
has got to give! Neither you nor I can afford to let today's biblical

"second spring" in the Church just pass us by. We dare not stand still. We cannot stand pat on that good old seminary scripture course. The Church is on the march—and I mean the whole Church. Today's biblical movement is not just the esoteric enthusiasm of a few scholars or specialists in the ivory towers of the Church. It *is* trickling down! It is permeating the whole mass of the Church. The laity are definitely alert to it. Something new is happening to our Catholic people. They are beginning to show signs of an insatiable interest in the Bible.

Recently in our parish we announced an adult Bible class to meet for one hour on Sunday mornings. We thought that we would be lucky indeed to get nine or ten to give an extra hour on Sunday morning in addition to Mass. More than five times that number registered for the class and attended faithfully. This is only one of many indices; I am sure you could cite others. It is safe to say that the Catholic faithful are more interested in the Bible today than at any other time in the long history of the Church. You and I are their teachers. We are their leaders. One day Mahatma Ghandi was resting inside a friend's house when a large crowd of people streamed past on the road outside. The great man rose quickly, pulled his robe about him and started out the door. "Where are you going," asked his host. "Those are my people," he said, "I must hurry and catch up with them—I am their leader." Fathers, those are our people who are turning with such avid interest to the Bible. We are their leaders. We must hurry and catch up with them. We must not only read about the Bible—with utter faith we must read the Bible. "*Tolle et lege*"!

The second reason why the study and use of the Bible thrusts itself upon us priests with special urgency today is the provision in the Constitution on the Sacred Liturgy which calls for the direct reading in the vernacular of the Scripture lessons at Mass. The dimensions of this reform far exceed a mere change in language. It is weighted with opportunity and challenge. It will be upon us shortly. We must be ready to exploit it. We must not fritter it away.

The Scripture readings are not just a nice trimming to pad out the Mass. They are integral to the Mass. The Constitution says: "The two parts which . . . go to make up the Mass, namely the liturgy of the word and the eucharistic liturgy, are so closely connected . . . that they form but one single act of worship" (Par. 56). The Eucharistic liturgy is the renewal of the New Covenant in the blood of the Lord. The liturgy of the word is the proclamation of the New Covenant in the words of the Lord. Before God's redeemed people renew their response to his covenanting act, he wishes them to make their response to his covenanting word. This was as God wanted it the very first time he called his chosen people into assembly at Sinai. This is as God wants it every Sunday as he calls his new chosen people into assembly in your parish church and in mine. It is for a dual purpose that he summons them there: he means for them to hear what he says, and he means for them to recall and renew what he does. In both instances he invites them to a response. At its deepest point, this is what the Christian life is all about: to make a response to God. A response to the saving words of God and a response to the saving acts of God.

The Scripture readings and homily are an integral part of that "one single act of worship," the Mass. It is here (and here only) that God speaks to his *ecclesia,* to his people assembled. They listen to all kinds of talk throughout the week: from their children, from their wives, from their husbands, from their friends and associates, from the television set. In the immortal words of Hamlet: "Words, words, words"! All week long they who are God's own people hear all kinds of talk—but none from God. Here, now, for these few precious moments, they have their one and only opportunity to hear *him* talk to them. What they hear now *is* God's word. What you read to them here is what God means now to say to them. Most of them never read the Bible, but even if they do we know that the written word cannot match the power of the spoken word, especially the power of the divine word spoken in the context of liturgical worship. God their Father means for them to *hear* it. He means for them to hear it spoken with conviction and authority and faith, so that "hearing the word they may keep it with a noble and generous heart, and endure, and yield a harvest" (Luke 8:15).

You administer the sacraments to the Christian people, but it is Christ who acts. You read God's word to his people, but it is God who acts to elicit their response. It is not that you speak for him to the assembly; rather he uses you to speak himself to the assembly. What exacting care you should bring to this exalted role! That badly mauled axiom *"ex opere operato"* tells you that, in a sense, in the sacraments God does not have to limit his power to act according to how you do them—but here, in a sense, he does! Here the *"opus operantis"* is incontrovertibly decisive. Their response to God's word depends very much on how you communicate his word to them. It is you they hear, but it is God who speaks. This is not your word you utter here; this is God's word. How profoundly aware you should be at this point of the power that pulses out through you upon those who hear you: it is none other than the power of the living God! What issues forth from you here is the living word of God—that word which does not return to him empty.

Dare you for a moment forget that it is the same word which once called the universe into being? "By the word of the Lord the heavens were made . . . Let all the earth fear the Lord, for he spoke and it was made" (Ps. 32). This word that goes out here from your lips can not only *move* mountains, it *made* them! Certainly it can move men and make faith. "God's word to us," said Paul, "is something alive, full of energy; it can penetrate deeper than any two-edged sword" (Heb. 4:12). In the first reading (which with some imprecision we call "the epistle") God speaks to his people in the inspired words of the Holy Spirit through the pen of Paul or Peter or Luke or James. In the gospel reading he speaks to them in the words of his own Son. We should change our little introduction from "At that time Jesus said . . ." to "At this time Jesus says . . ." "God who at different times and in various ways spoke in times past to our fathers by the prophets . . . in these days has spoken to us by his Son" (Heb. 1:1).

For so long now this dramatic presence of God among his as-sembled people has been obscured by the incredible spectacle of a spokesman with his back to those whom he "addresses," speak-ing to them in a language understood not at all by them and frequently not even by him! At Sunday Mass we have tried to save the day by interrupting the action, turning around in the right direction and re-delivering God's word in a language God's people can understand. But somehow it is not quite what it should be and not at all what it could be. It is warmed-over, second-hand. The impact is blunted. The freshness is gone.

Now this is to be changed. Thanks to the Constitution on the Sacred Liturgy, you will shortly deliver God's word to his people face to face in their language in the one liturgical action.

Are you ready for it? In what manner are you going to let God speak to his people? Faith comes by hearing—especially by hearing God speak. God's people have only one opportunity of hearing God speak to them: by listening to you deliver his word at Sunday Mass. By what he says to them here, God means to elicit a response from them. Are you going to block that response by the way you have him say what he has to say? By what he says to them here, God means to awaken, revive and nurture their faith. Are you going to cheat them out of what God means to give them by the way you have him say what he has to say?

Perhaps nothing is so important for you and me as our own

faith in what we do here. *Agnoscite quod agitis!* You are very
careful with the words of consecration at Mass. It is with utter
reverence you handle the Sacred Host and the chalice. You com-
port yourself with real dignity. Why? Because you are deeply
aware, as you take up that bread and cup at the consecration
that the Lord is truly present in what you do there. Because you
have faith in what you do there. And because you *have* this faith
you also *give* faith to God's people who observe you in awed silence.
I ask you, should your faith in what you do in the scripture lessons
be any less intense? Is your faith in the Lord's real presence there
forgotten or obscured? You do believe, as you take up that bread
and cup, that the Lord is really and truly present in what you
do there. Do you not believe, as you take up that book, that the
Lord is really and truly present in what you do there also? The
Constitution on the Sacred Liturgy says: "(At Mass) Christ is
present in his word, since it is he himself who speaks when the
holy scriptures are read in the Church" (Par. 7). Yes, "Christ is
present in his word" as you and I deliver it here to his brethren.
You and I must have faith in what we do at Mass—not only at
the consecration but also at the scripture readings. The Lord Jesus
Christ is really and truly present in the Mass: not only in the
liturgy of the Eucharist but also in the liturgy of the word.

Before God can use us to *give* faith in these two modes of the
Lord's real presence we have to *have* faith in his real presence.
And if we have this faith it will show in the very way in which
we do these things: *sancta sancte!* This faith of ours shows through
with irresistible cogency at the consecration. Our whole bearing
must project it with the same power at the scripture readings: in
such ordinary things as the way we pick up the Book of the
New Covenant, in the way we handle it, in the way we read it
aloud to God's people, in the way we close it and return it to
its place. Yes, faith comes by hearing. And to each of us is offered
the grace of actually experiencing the truth of this—Sunday after

Sunday as we read the word of God to the people of God. Even
in this second-hand way we must now do it, there is something
almost charismatic about our reading of the scriptures in church—
an effect which will certainly be heightened when we read God's
word to his people in the one liturgical action. This never ceases
to astound me. I think it is one of the great moments of our ministry. Faith comes by hearing, and as we read the scriptures to
them we can see this faith come alive in the very faces of those
people as they listen. And how hungrily, how eagerly they do
listen! Their attention is uncanny. Their response is almost palpable. Happening here before our eyes we see what he meant
when he said "my word shall not return to me empty." We see
proven all over again that indeed "man does not live by bread
alone but by every word that proceeds from the mouth of God."
Before our very eyes we see the mighty and mysterious power
of God's living word. We can sense that power as it goes out
from us—*virtus ab illo exibat!*

In our parish we have never been able to get our people to
respond *"Laus tibi, Christe"* at the end of the gospel in the latin
dialog Mass. It has always been ragged and weak and desultory
and unfelt. But if we do the forthcoming direct reading in the
vernacular with a living faith in the Lord's real presence in this
word of his we send out to his people, I promise you that we
shall also give them faith that he *is* present and has spoken personally to them. If you and I can bring this kind of faith to the
scripture readings of the Mass, they will elicit a true response in
faith. We shall hear, rising from their grateful hearts, the full-
throated cry: "Praise be to you, O Christ"! Praise be to you really
present here and working in your living word which we have
just heard and which we will keep "with a noble and generous
heart, and endure, a yield a harvest . . . All that you have said,
Lord, we will heed and do."

7. "Ephphetha, be opened"— The Signs of Faith

THE LITURGICAL MOVEMENT has not always moved in the right direction. There is a growing suspicion that we may, in the immediate past, have overemphasized the necessity of interiorization. In 1947, Pius XII reminded us in *Mediator Dei* that "the chief element of divine worship must be interior" (Par. 24) and warned against the error of "thinking of the sacred liturgy as merely the outward part of divine worship" (Par. 25). Because for so long liturgy had been confused with mere rubrics, these cautionary words were not only welcome but necessary 'way back in the pioneering days of 1947. Perhaps we heeded them not wisely but too well. To free itself from the stigma of equating liturgy with the externals of worship, the liturgical movement bent over backwards to emphasize the interior aspects of true worship. Perhaps we bent too far too fast. We may have gone to such pains to vindicate the validity of the internals that we forgot something of the value and validity of the externals in the sacred liturgy. Perhaps the time has come in the liturgical movement to stop apologizing for the fact that we are Catholics and not Quakers.

After all, the sacred liturgy exists in the world of *signs*. And signs are first of all gloriously and unabashedly *external*. Catholic theology does not say that the sacraments cause grace. Catholic theology says that the sacraments cause grace *because they are signs: "significando causant gratiam."* The interior reality is integrally and essentially related to the external sign. In the liturgy, signs are not merely important, they are essential. Let us be forthright about it: without prejudice to the internals, the externals of the sacred liturgy have a relevance that is absolutely indispensable.

Let us also make a confession: our present-day liturgical sign-making leaves something to be desired in the context of present-day life. There is nothing more pathetic than a sign which does not signify. The sign which has to be explained is not a good sign. We have many signs in our liturgy today which need to be explained to be understood. Anointing with oil, eating salt, imposing hands and speaking in Latin were once-upon-a-time magnificent signs. Nobody had to explain them or interpret them. Their meaning was obvious. Their power of signification was immediate. Once-upon-a-time yes, but not today. There is nothing treasonable in admitting this—the Church, through Vatican II, has admitted it and in the Constitution on the Sacred Liturgy has called for revision and reform of much of the liturgy and has asked that "in this restoration, both texts and rites should be drawn up so that they express more clearly the holy things which they signify" (Par. 21).

But let us make the confession complete: we who use them have not made the most of the signs the liturgy gives us. The old proverb remains valid: he is a poor workman who blames his tools. Before we scream too loudly about the signs the liturgy gives us, let each of us ask how well he has used them.

"Faith comes by hearing." But if the sacred liturgy teaches us anything it teaches that faith also comes *by seeing: significando causant gratiam!* In the sacraments God causes grace, gives and sustains faith, not only by what the people hear but also by what they see and observe.

Whatever else he may be, each of us is a liturgist—he *does* the sacred liturgy; well, badly or indifferently, he does it. Each of us engages regularly in sacred sign-making as he celebrates the liturgy in his parish. It is superfluous to remind ourselves that this sign-making is the most important activity any of us has. Between us we must have a vast store of practice and experience. Let us share it. Let us explore together practical ways of more effectively using the external signs given us by the Lord and by his Church in the sacred liturgy we celebrate.

Let us begin with baptism: the great sacrament of Christian initiation, of first call and first response, of first grace and first faith. The Eucharist is the new covenant, but it is in baptism that God makes the new covenant with each of his adopted children.

(The following is an edited report of replies contributed by priests during several retreats:)

▶ "Before I begin I always give a brief talk on the purpose and meaning of Christian baptism and an explanation of the major themes of the rite itself: call and response, death and resurrection, the covenant with its twin aspects of promise and obligation. Nor do I hesitate to interject short commentaries on certain of the signs as they occur during the rite: the insufflation, giving the salt, the *aperitio aurium,* both anointings, the turning-from and turning-to of the baptism vow, the giving of the white garment and lighted candle. So it takes 30 minutes instead of 15. But I have yet to hear anyone complain. The liturgy is our best teacher—if we help it along just a little."

▶ "I force myself to take my time. If we hurry through the rite in 12 minutes it is pretty hard to convince anyone present that something big is happening. There is no substitute for dignity and conviction on the part of the minister. Of all the wonderful signs God uses to give the faith as I administer baptism, none can be more effective or more destructive than myself. And we should reflect that baptism gives faith not only to the subject but also to the "circumstantes." Baptism ranks with First Communion in its ability to touch the heart and stir the lagging faith of a proud daddy or mother—if we do it right."

► "We keep handy a supply of the Liturgical Press booklets containing the Rite of Baptism. Everyone present (including non-Catholics) is given one of these booklets and invited not merely to follow along but to participate vocally wherever this is indicated."

► "Ladies of the parish gladly keep us supplied with the white garments and candles used in the rite. The garments are simply made of white linen, and both the garments and candles are hand-decorated with appropriate baptismal symbols. We actually clothe the newly baptized child in the garment and give him this and the candle as his first present from the family into which he has just been born—the family of God. We ask the parents to keep these meaningful souvenirs for the child and to explain them to him before First Holy Communion. It is amazing how grateful and how impressed the parents are by this—and not just the mothers but the fathers too."

► "In our parish we also give newly baptized infants the white garment, but for adult converts we substitute a kind of white stole. We ask them to wear this symbol of their baptismal integrity every year at the parish Easter Vigil service, and it is heartening to see the number of white stoles increase year after year."

► "We keep the left-over paschal candle in the baptistry and we light the baptismal candle from this primary sign of the risen Christ, the light of the world, before giving it to the newly Christ-ened."

Signs, however good in themselves, are simply no good if there is nobody to see them. The sign-boards most in demand are those at the busiest intersections; the highest-priced television time is in the evening hours when the sponsors' signs are most likely to be seen and heard. The rite of baptism is an extraordinarily effective sign but it is seen by so few. Except the Eucharist, none of the sacraments is more "ecclesial" than baptism, but in actual practice none except Penance has become more "private." More often than not, nobody is present except the baby, the sponsors and the parents, and sometimes not even the parents bother to come. In an effort to counteract this we try to schedule baptisms at a time most convenient to our people, and we encourage them to plan a baptism party in their homes and to invite the guests not just to the cocktails but to the ceremony. Without having to say so, this also helps impress upon them that baptism is a truly festive occasion.

It was when I made a Cursillo that I resolved to try to do something not only about *receiving* adult converts into the Church but about *welcoming* them into the Church. The closing of this Cursillo was one of the more memorable religious experiences of my life. As we new Cursillistas walked out of chapel that Sunday night we were met by hundreds of veteran Cursillistas who lined the sidewalk for the better part of a city block and who had come here from their homes and TV sets just to welcome us into the ranks. The warmth and exuberance of their greeting was patently sincere and unaffected. I am no sentimentalist but this thing really overwhelmed me. Both during the Cursillo but especially now, for possibly the first time, I experienced "*koinonia*"—real Christian fellowship. Later that night a layman from our parish, himself a convert, who had made the Cursillo with us, jolted me by asking "Father, could you imagine the people of our parish coming out like that to welcome a newly baptized convert into the Church with that kind of enthusiasm?" Frankly, I could not. But neither could I keep from asking myself "Why not? Why couldn't they? Why shouldn't they?" We have lost something in the Church, something big, something important. We are cold, impersonal, insular. Where is our vaunted "bond of unity?" The genius of the Cursillo movement is that it re-discovers "*koinonia*." Rather, it enables our Catholic people to discover it for the first time in their lives, after years in the Church. This electrifying discovery, which should have been theirs all along, explains the magic of the Cursillo.

We Christians had it once. It is in the New Testament we find evidence of it. For the apostles, and especially for Paul, "*koinonia*" expressed the very essence of Christianity: fellowship with God, and with one another in God. Perhaps we have been entirely too fatuous in our easy contempt of Protestantism's preoccupation with "fellowship." Perhaps we would do well to begin to suspect that the loneliness of the ruggedly individualistic "me and Jesus" kind of religion is not only unChristian but inhuman as well. This sense of Christian fellowship should be strongest in the celebration of the Eucharist (what else does "Communion" mean?), but there is room for it in the other sacraments too, especially the sacrament of baptism. God hasten the day when not just the Christian minister but the Christian community will present itself for the encounter with God in Christ which baptism is, so that the great prayers of baptism will be truly and visibly the prayers of the Church for this new member of the family. If the Church is the people of God, it is more than fitting that the people of God be present more than by proxy when the Church gives a sacrament, especially the sacrament of initiation.

Now let us confer about our celebration of the parish Eucharist. All of us, I suppose, talk about "the Church" dozens of times in the course of any normal week—in our instructions, sermons and just ordinary conversation. Invariably what we mean is the whole thing: the Church universal. But in the existential order, as event, when and where and what is "the church"—the actual, visible bodying-forth of the assembled people of God? It is on Sunday, in your parish church and mine, as our people assemble around the altar for Mass.

All of us engaged in the parish ministry talk about "the parish" very often. And invariably we talk about it and we think about it as a kind of administrative unit of the Church—as an ecclesiastical division born of the need for more efficient pastoral care. Indeed this is our view of "the diocese": a higher, larger and more important administrative unit of the Church.

Now there is nothing wrong with this kind of thinking—but not everything is right with it either. The parish is much more than this, and the diocese is much, much more. Each in its own right is "the church." In Ephesians Paul wrote, "(Christ is) the head to which the *whole* Church is joined, so that the Church is his body . . ." (Eph. 1:23). Indeed the whole Church, the Church universal, is the body of Christ. But this did not prevent Paul from telling the Christian community at Corinth, "*You* are Christ's body" (I Cor. 12:27). In his epistles St. Paul does use the word "church" to mean the universal Church, but more often he uses it to designate the Christian community of some particular place or city, as, for instance, "the Church of God which is at Corinth" (II Cor. 1:1). Indeed he even uses the word occasionally to designate a community of Christians gathered together in a private home to celebrate the Eucharist, e.g. "Greet Nymphas, with the church that is in his household" (Col. 4:15). And it is interesting to count the number of times the plural, "churches," occurs in the New Testament, especially in the Pauline and Johannine writings.

There is a mystery and a wholeness about Sunday Mass in your parish. It is the very mystery of the Church. It is the wholeness of the whole Christ. Your parish is truly exceptional if it is aware of this. "The Church" exists not only in the wide, wide world—it exists also in your parish every Sunday. In a sense, this is the *only* way the Church exists. Karl Rahner says, "The Church, as event, is *necessarily* a local and localized community." The Church, as actualized and visible event, exists only in the priest and people assembled together in unity around the parish altar by the Word of God and the Body of Christ. It is here the Eucharist is celebrated— something so great that the whole Church universal can do nothing greater.

Father, how dreadfully casual we are about Sunday Mass in our parishes! Most of us regard it as another item on an overloaded agenda. In theory not one of us doubts or denies its primary importance. But in practice we do not regard it as a particularly urgent challenge to our pastoral ingenuity. It is pretty well set; it rolls along smoothly enough and lays no pressing claim upon our thought or attention. Father, let me tell you this: nothing presents a greater challenge to you as a priest than Sunday Mass in your parish. Nothing is more important for our Christian people than their full and proper participation in Sunday Mass. Nothing is more difficult for them.

My own highest ambition before I die is to get just one parish congregation to offer just one Sunday Mass with me as Sunday Mass should be offered. The achievement of this ambition is nowhere in sight. Every Sunday during Mass you say these grand words to God the Father about this church assembled around you at the altar: "... *quorum tibi fides cognita est et nota devotio*— whose total personal commitment (*fides*) and complete self-surrender (*devotio*) are known to you." Nothing is more important for these Christian people than that those words should ring true. Nothing is more difficult for them than to make them ring true. Nothing you and I can do for them is more important than to help them make those words ring true. Nothing you and I try to do for them is more difficult. And all the while we are rather casual about Sunday Mass. With a sigh of relief we are grateful to let Sunday Mass take care of itself—while we are busy about many things. "*Porro unum est necessarium*"! Fathers, something big and basic is wrong when a sincere priest spends more time and thought and

energy on how to make the Altar Society click or how to make the
Fund Drive click than on how to make Sunday Mass click. Something is haywire if we are more concerned about the parish school
than about the parish Mass. Each of us has got to realize that
nothing, absolutely nothing, is more worthy of his pastoral care
than Sunday Mass in his parish. Let us confer together on how we
can make Sunday Mass the central and ultimate act of worship it is
meant to be: the true expression of the "*fides et devotio*" of God's
holy people.

(The following is an edited report of statements contributed by
priests during several retreats.)

▶ "Before introducing the Dialogue Mass in our parish, we explained the 1958 Instruction during the course of several weeks'
sermons to convince our people that it was not just their parish
priests but the Church herself who wants and expects their vocal
participation. We then printed our own Dialogue Mass cards for
congregational use and introduced the people to them gradually,
providing opportunity for rehearsal before every Mass. It was hard
and slow work, but they knew we meant business and now at
least seventy-five to eighty percent of them participate in the full
Dialogue Mass readily and enthusiastically. Two or three times
during the year we devote our sermon time to refresher instructions
to prevent their participation becoming merely external."

▶ "We got tired of fighting the battle of the Latin. We switched
to singing—in English. Our people now answer only the short
responses and say only the *Pater Noster* and *Domine non sum
dignus* in Latin. They pray the Apostles' Creed in English during
the celebrant's Nicene Creed. All the rest of their vocal participation
is by pertinent vernacular hymns: at the Kyrie, Offertory, Sanctus,
Agnus Dei and Communion. They also sing appropriate English
hymns at the beginning and end of Mass as the celebrant and

servers walk down the center aisle in procession. The words and notes of these hymns are printed on special cards. We change these three or four times a year. One of our first hurdles is to restore a sense of community to our Sunday congregations. Congregational singing is one of the best tools at our disposal. Too many of us are afraid to use it. We underestimate our people's ability and willingness to sing in church. They will do it if we tell them why and show them how."

► "I trained several of the men of our parish to lead the congregation in the dialogue Mass. I bought them copies of Father Howell's book of Mass commentaries to help the people follow the entire action more intelligently. These commentaries are brief and to the point. Our people know that there is a time for sound and a time for silence during Mass."

► "We are fortunate not to have a choir loft in our parish church. For Sunday High Mass our choir occupies the front pews and the director and organist are in full view. One Sunday each month the choir sings a full figured Mass; on the others the choir itself does only the "propers" and an Offertory and Communion motet, while the entire congregation joins them in the "ordinary" parts. We use "People's Mass" cards from the World Library of Sacred Music and our people have proudly mastered a repertoire of three of these Masses. They like it—and it can be done"!

► "I had a portable altar custom-made to stand at the entrance to the sanctuary. Occasionally, both on weekdays and Sundays, we move this altar into place and celebrate Holy Mass facing the people. The bond between altar, celebrant and congregation is visibly heightened. Our people tell us again and again that the Mass "means" so much more to them this way."

▶ "I try to make the Mass gestures meaningful. When we greet them at the *"Dominus vobiscum"* why must we hold our hands as though we are wrapping yarn or measuring a cigar box? I extend my hands in greeting. And if we expect them to respond *"Et cum spiritu tuo"* with any meaning at all, why must we give the impression of spurning their response by turning *immediately* to the missal? I pause the few seconds it takes for them to make their response. I believe in letting them see that I await it and expect it. And when we pray to the Father in their name during the Collect, Secret and Post-Communion, why not let the position of our hands bespeak petition? They cannot understand what we are saying but they should understand what we are doing. The new *"ritus servandus"* says simply that we are to position our hands *"ante pectus."* I do not interpret that rubric as forbidding us to assume a position indicative of real pleading."

▶ "The Communion procession is the only one not taken away from our people in Sunday Mass. But in practice we have taken this one away from them too. It has been my experience that in most of our parish churches it is more of a stampede than a procession. In our parish church everyone remains kneeling until after the third people's *"Domine non sum dignus."* At this point everybody stands. This not only dramatizes the fact that Holy Communion somehow involves the *entire* congregation, but serves the prosaically practical purpose of eliminating communicants having to stumble over the legs of kneeling non-communicants. Communicants in the front pews walk immediately to the Communion table by way of the center aisle and return by way of the side aisles. Communicants in succeeding pews walk out into the center aisle to form an honest-to-goodness Communion procession. Nothing we do in our parish church at Sunday Mass impresses visitors more. And when any of our people go to Mass in another church on a given Sunday they invariably return to remark about the "disorderliness" encountered at Communion time."

▶ "The pastor installed microphone plugs in the front pew so that the lay readers can be clearly heard by everyone. We also have microphones in the altar gradines so that the celebrant can be heard by the entire congregation."

▶ "The priest at the altar not only makes sacred signs, he himself *is* a sacred sign. I think nothing is more important for that *"fides et devotio"* you mentioned than the way we "say Mass." And I think speed and routine are our worst enemies. Every year on retreat I try to get one of the priests to "check" me as I offer Holy Mass. Too many of us garble the sacred words and, in the true sense of the term, desecrate the sacred actions. I am not suggesting that we should dawdle at the altar or that we should play the pious fraud. But when we stand at the altar of sacrifice we should be living signs that we know what we are saying and that we mean what we are saying. Even if the people cannot understand what we are saying, they can understand whether or not we understand what we are saying—and what we are doing. There should be a genuine sense of the holy about all our actions and gestures as we celebrate Holy Mass. I know from personal experience that the urge to hurry and the attrition of repetition present an unending challenge to every one of us."

8. "Making hope live in us"—
Priestly Hope

"THE JUST MAN lives by faith"—and every man lives by hope. No man can live without hope. Man cannot survive without hope at least of some kind, at least in some one or in some thing. In your pastoral ministry as you have gone about visiting the sick and dying of your parish you have probably heard more than once something like this: "Papa is going to die now; he has given up hope." And how true this is! When the hope of living is gone, a man simply cannot go on living. There literally is nothing left to live for.

This is true of hope not only in the natural order but also in the supernatural order. When God gave you his life at baptism, he also gave you the virtue of hope. This is as it should be, because it would be impossible for you to go on living the supernatural *life* without supernatural *hope*. There would have been absolutely no point in God giving you the one without the other. "The just man lives by faith"; but make no mistake about it, he also lives by hope.

Christian hope is almost the forgotten virtue. Hope gets much less attention than faith or charity. To scan our literature or to monitor our sermons is almost to get the impression that there is a conspiracy of silence against the theological virtue of hope in comparison with the other two. This is more than passing strange in view of our conviction that hope is every bit as essential to salvation as faith or charity. One were tempted to remark "God help you if you lose hope"—until he reflects that when you do indeed lose hope not even God can help you. It behooves us, Father, to return Christian hope to its proper place in the Christian life.

There is a clear and present danger in any attempt to analyze Christian hope: the danger of bogging down in the "tyranny of the it." It is the danger of making hope merely a thing. To speak of "the virtue of hope" is immediately to confirm this. Christian hope is not something about something. Hope is utterly personal: a person's relation to a Person. Hope is you and God. Hope is your way of saying "in God I trust." Unquestioning trust, confidence, expectancy is the dynamic of hope. The Christian hopes not merely *in* God, he hopes to *have* God. The dynamic of Christian hope, firmly rooted in persons, is the expectation of heaven.

Father, something has happened either to our hope or to our grasp of its implications. Our expectancy of heaven is hidden under a bushel. What is the image we Catholics, laity and clergy, present to the world about us? It is the image of a people awash in a sense of its own sinfulness: *"Nobis quoque peccatoribus* . . . Pray for us sinners now and at the hour of our death . . . " It is the image of a people uncertain of heaven, morbidly fearful of losing eternal happiness, confused and ominously silent about the hope that lives in us. We are mealy-mouthed about going to heaven, and we talk instead about being lucky to make it to purgatory. The passion, resurrection and ascension did not happen in order to get us to purgatory; they happened in order to get us to heaven—"in order that where I am there you also may be." But we are ridden by the ghosts of fear and diffidence and we scarcely dare open our mouths about heaven. Presumption or cockiness is bad indeed—but pessimism and faintheartedness is worse. An unhealthy defeatism immobilizes and demoralizes us. This from *us*! From us who at our baptism were assured over and over again ". . . that you may have everlasting life." This from us who have received the Spirit of adoption which makes us cry out "Abba, Father"! This from us whom the Spirit himself assures that we are the sons of God and, because we are sons, enjoying the son's right of inheritance! (Cfr. Romans 8:15-17)

It was not always thus. Our modern Catholic morbidity about purgatory and hell was not the message of the New Covenant. The early Church pulsated with hope. When our Lord sent his apostles out to preach, it was not merely "news" they were to herald. Significantly, it was GOOD news! "Preach the Gospel to every creature"—the good, good news of the kingdom of heaven. Hope of everlasting happiness was the quintessence of the Christian gospel. Hope was more than the theme of the apostles' preaching: it was the very purpose and goal of that preaching. "The hope of what awaits you in heaven," said Paul, "was the lesson you learned from that truth-giving message of the gospel which has reached you, which now bears fruit and thrives in you . . . since you heard of God's grace and recognized it for what it is" (Col. 1:4-6). Note carefully what St. Paul said: ". . . hope was *the* lesson you learned from that truth-giving message of the gospel." This was echoed by St. Peter: "Blessed be God, the Father of our Lord Jesus Christ, who in his great mercy has begotten us anew, *making hope live in us* through the resurrection of Jesus Christ from the dead . . . We are to share an inheritance that is incorruptible . . . It is stored up for you *in heaven,* and meanwhile, through your faith, the power of God affords you safe conduct until you reach it" (I Peter 1:3-5).

What is most significant about these and similar passages is not so much what the Holy Spirit says about hope and about the expectancy of heaven, but what he says about *why* Christians have this hope. The Christians of that time had this hope because they REMEMBERED. They were intensely aware of the saving acts of God; they remembered how God had loved them . . . "Blessed be God"! Under the sure guidance of the apostles, their eyes were on

God rather than on themselves and on their sinfulness. Notice what St. Paul said in the passage quoted. The Colossians had this hope, a hope of heaven bearing fruit and thriving in them, "since they heard of God's grace and recognized it for what it is." Have we not here the reason for our diffidence? We too have heard of God's grace, but do we recognize it for what it is? Are we so steeped in our own stinginess that we cannot recognize God's magnanimity for what it is? And notice what St. Peter said about the "hope that lives in us . . . the hope of an incorruptible inheritance stored up for us in heaven." The reason it is a living and dynamic hope is precisely "the resurrection of Jesus Christ from the dead." It remains a living and dynamic hope because "*the power of God* affords you safe conduct until you reach it." The focus throughout is on God, not on the sinful Christian. God does not open the gates of heaven to you and then, as it were, let you sink or swim. By his power, by his grace, he *leads* you to its fulfillment. Hope of heaven is always and only hope in God. When your eyes are fixed on yourself you encounter a weakness and infidelity all too obvious and, of course, you wax fearful. Look to God! Remember his past saving acts and his present grace. Under the spiritual direction of the apostles, this was what the Christians of their day did. They left behind a record of Christian hope which in its sheer exuberance almost scandalizes us today: "We stand confident in the hope of attaining glory . . . nor does this hope delude us." How long since any of us has talked like that! How different this sounds from the timorous and wishy-washy hope which characterizes us today. They had this hope and we do not have it because they remember and we do not remember. "We were reconciled to God through his Son's death and, so reconciled, we are surer than ever of finding salvation" (Rom. 5:10). They remembered that God had loved them so much he sent his own Son to be an atonement for their sins. "Christ never knew sin, and God made him into sin for us, so that in him we might be turned into the holiness of God" (II Cor. 5:21). They remembered that God's love for them personally had called them to baptism and incorporation into Christ sacrificed, risen and ascended, so that Christ's death was also their acquittal from sin, Christ's resurrection was also their resurrection, Christ's ascension was also their ascension. "Just as all have died with Adam, so with Christ all will be brought to life" (I Cor. 15:22). "It is God's grace that has saved you; raised us up too, enthroned us too above the heavens in Christ Jesus" (Eph. 2:6). Under the deft touch of the apostles the Christians of that day saw that grace was truly grace, "recognized it for what it was." They saw that "justification comes to us as a free gift from God's grace . . . that where sin abounded, grace did more abound" (Rom. 3:24 and 5:20). And so they could say: "We stand confident in the hope of attaining glory; nor does this hope delude us."

Such, Father, was the heritage of hope bequeathed us. What happened to it? A good monk, a well-meaning monk, wrecked it. His name was Pelagius. He has been dead more than fifteen hundred years. But what he started is not dead by a long shot. As you know, Pelagius taught that real original sin does not really exist, that grace is not necessary, that man can merit heaven all by himself. That mighty warrior, Augustine, annihilated the Pelagian doctrine; and the Church, in the person of Pope Boniface II, quickly and decisively condemned it. But pride dies a slow death, and the Pelagian heresy in essence is pride: man's pride in his own prowess, man's cocky assurance that he can pull himself up to heaven by his own bootstraps. As a matter of fact, in this case pride does not die slowly—it simply refuses to die. The Pelagian heresy, under one fancy guise or another, is still very much alive and kicking today. Under the guise of our one-sided insistence on the necessity of personal "good works" it was at least partially responsible for triggering the Protestant Reformation. Under the thin guise of our tendency to overstate what we must personally do to gain eternal salvation, at the expense of understating what God has done to give us eternal salvation, we must confess the insidious persistence of the Pelagian poison in our midst even to this day. In the practical order we today simply refuse to come to grips with the doctrine of grace. Listen to our sermons and read our spiritual books: note the preoccupation (and almost total preoccupation) with what we must do to "merit" eternal salvation. Or listen to our Catholic people and to their bizarre notions about piling up merit like a savings account and thus insuring salvation.

How oblivious they are that in simple fact "nobody can come to me unless the Father who sent me draw him" (John 6:44). "Lord, what must I do to gain eternal life?" is still as pertinent a question as ever—but it must be predicated on a remembrance of what the Lord has done to give eternal life. We cannot throw off the fascination of old Pelagius' siren thesis that grace is not really necessary and that we can indeed somehow do it ourselves. This results inevitably in our half-hearted hope of eternal happiness. We look to ourselves rather than to God. Sooner or later we are confronted with the ugly fact of our inadequacy—and we are scared stiff. This spineless and wavering hope, characteristic of our modern Catholic piety, stems basically from our failure to remember what God in "his loving design" once did to redeem us and does now to save us.

This is not to imply that hope is synonymous with certainty. There is always the element of the possible in hope. Hope of attaining heaven does not exclude the possibility of losing heaven. If it did it would not be hope. You do not, for instance, hope that two plus two will add up to four. Hope is necessarily colored with the possibility of failure. If it be true hope, fear will always be present but will never predominate. The moment it does it *is* fear and not hope. Trust is the most typical element in hope—a trust which infallibly overcomes fear. And so, while hope is not cockiness or certainty, neither is it a shrinking violet: it is forthright, bold, assured expectancy. "We stand confident in the hope of attaining glory . . . We are surer than ever of finding salvation . . . Hope *lives* in us."

Father, I would invite you to rediscover the absolute indispensability of hope to your personal spiritual life. You must put first things first. I frankly confess that I remember precious little from my philosophy course in the seminary. But I think I recall something to the effect that end or purpose determines nature. What is the end or purpose of the "spiritual life?" It is to return you safely to God. All mystical and ascetical niceties aside, it is to get you to heaven. Whatever the "school," whatever the "system" (or with most of us, God help us, *lack* of system), it all boils down to this, does it not: its purpose is to get you to heaven. Under and with God's grace, *you* have to *do* something to get there. I ask you, what have you done or what are you doing to get to the planet Mars? Nothing, of course. You know, there is only one reason why you have not done anything to get there: you have *no hope* of getting there! Where hope is not active, there is no action. Not only is there none, there can be none. Hope of attainment not only precedes practical action: it is the *sine qua non* of practical action. And conversely, the more vital the hope, the more indefatigable and effective the practical activity.

Hope inevitably tends toward fulfillment. Let them tell you all they want about how to attain eternal happiness, of this you may be sure: you will not and you can not do anything at all to attain it unless you are moved by *hope* of attaining it. And of something else you may be sure: the more dynamic your hope, the more you can and will do to bring it to fulfillment. What we call the theological virtue of hope may not be the first step in the spiritual life—but without it you cannot take that first step. And if it be strong enough you will take the last step!

You know, Father, there is immense wisdom in the Church. Near the end of the seventeenth century, under the aegis of a pious Archbishop named François Fénelon, there appeared a "school" of far-out religious purists who taught that the "real McCoy" spirit-

uality was attained only when one acted solely out of love for God
without any admixture of self-seeking, even the enlightened self-
seeking of gaining eternal life. The only real act of love of God,
they said, was the one without any tinge of hope. The ultimate goal
in doing good works is to rise above the selfishness of hope. Do
you know what the Church said about that "highfaluting spiritual
malarky?" Pope Innocent XII, in the brief *"Cum alias"*, vindicated
for all time the likes of unspiritual, selfish types like you and me by
labeling this teaching, and I quote: ". . . temerarious, scandalous,
male sonans, offensive to pious ears, pernicious and erroneous" (Cfr.
Denzinger, 1327–1349). Ah, Father, what a blow was struck there
for common-sense, down-to-earth spirituality! The Church has
fiercely defended the truth that your hope of eternal happiness is
somehow behind every good act you perform, even behind those
you *think* are inspired by utterly selfless love of God and neighbor.
Father, you cannot divorce hope from *anything* you do in the
supernatural order. Wisely, the Church long ago chose the anchor
as the symbol of Christian hope. This *is* the anchor, the foundation,
of your personal spirituality.

And it is the foundation of the spirituality of your people too.
Hope is the only thing that will keep them going—and they get it
only through you! Those wonderful people to whom you and I
are sent to minister: steeped in materialism, selfish and apathetic
and contentious, but withal somehow innately noble, generous,
grand, good—the devoted, anxious mother; the hard-working,
lovable guy of a father; God's holy people all. Father, at heart they
are beat down, frightened, insecure. What they need most in all the
world is hope: they hunger for it, seek it, crave it. It is their birthright. God their Father gave it to them at their baptism—every
mother's son and daughter of them. For some inscrutable reason
God depends on you to keep it alive in them. As once he depended
on the apostles to light the self-same spark of hope in those who

heard them, so does he now depend on you. God lights the flame, but you must bear it aloft for them to see and follow. You keep hope alive in them by giving them the sacraments, by offering the sacrifice for them and with them, by your preaching, by the witness of your priestly life. You must never, never give them the impression or allow them to get the impression that your own hope of eternal happiness has the wobbles or the shakes. If you do, you may be proud of your humility but they are scandalized—"Gee, Father, if you are so uncertain about getting to heaven, what chance is there for me?" You may not believe in yourself, but you have got to believe in them believing in you. Their Christian hope leans on yours. It must be there for them to lean on: not cockily flaunted but quiet, strong, calmly assured and genuine.

As a brash young priest I once made the mistake of giving a retreat to a community of semi-cloistered nuns. Their average age was roughly that of my great-grandmother. I do not know what it was for those dear old Sisters, but for me it proved to be one of the most unnerving and shocking experiences of my life. During the course of that retreat several of these saintly women, in the twilight of a lifetime of consecrated service in the house of the Lord, approached me in private conference shedding bitter tears over the almost certain prospect that they were headed straight for hell! I have never forgotten this. It was weird. It left me, as the little boy says, "all shook up." And yet, Father, do not we priests do something of the same thing to our poor people when, either in jest or in earnest, we disclaim in their presence the hope of heaven that is in us?

And what of the scandal that all of us who are the Church, clergy and laity, unwittingly cause to those outside? The image we present to the world is not the image of a people "standing confident in the hope of attaining glory . . . surer than ever of finding salvation." It is the image of a people more cowed by fear than borne up by hope.

Jean Danielou says, "It is not the world that doubts Christians, but Christians who no longer believe in themselves." I cannot help but think that the miracle of converting the world wrought by the early Christians resulted not only from the witness of their charity but also from the witness of their hope. Every man seeks security. Every man is totally engaged in the pursuit of happiness. What every man is looking for is hope. We who are the Church have what they are looking for. But we hide it from them! We prefer a discreet and judicious and inconspicuous hope—and meanwhile the Communists are bidding fair to win the world. They are not winning it by force of arms. It is not altogether an oversimplification to say they are winning it by the promise of hope. It is the hope of heaven, the hope of a heaven-on-earth: to build here a society without class distinctions and without poverty. Do you object that this is a natural hope? That it is in fact a false hope? Why yes. But that is not the point: they are winning and we are not and it may well be that the proffered hope is what makes the difference.

Finally, let us try to see that, as priests, we must not only give hope to our people, we must also have hope in our people. Just as in the case of faith, so too in the case of hope is there a social character which must not be ignored. Christian hope, no less than Christian faith, is *social*. There is nothing private or individualistic about the origin of supernatural hope in you. You got it with First Grace—and you got First Grace by incorporation into a community called the Church which is the Body of Christ. This hope which lives in you is a sharing: a sharing in the hope of the Church. Your hope, therefore, is essentially communal in its origin.

Your hope is also essentially communal in its orientation. What you hope for is to be attained not in isolation, but only in living adherence in a Body made up of many with Christ as its Head. "I am the way . . . nobody can come to the Father except through me" (John 14:6). It is only by incorporation into the Church that you get

hope—and only so that you keep it and exercise it and bring it to
fulfillment. Christian hope is essentially corporate. It is the Church
who hopes to return to the Father; it is the Church which is the
Body of Christ which ascends into heaven. Your hope of heaven is
a living expression of the Church's hope of heaven. This precious
hope of yours is not any kind of reward for belonging to the Church,
it is proper to your very condition as being the Church. You hope
to go to heaven only because the Church hopes to go to heaven. The
Church is the people of God: the very people to whom you have
been sent to minister. This people is a people in pilgrimage: this
people is on its way back to the Father. The definitive return to the
Father, the final consummation of Christian hope will be gloriously
communal: at the *Parousia* when all of us together and no one alone
shall return in Christ to the Father.

For us priests this is a truth of the first order. It is this precisely
which forms the basis of pastoral zeal. Pastoral zeal denotes an
abiding concern for the spiritual well-being of those under one's
care. More specifically it denotes an expressed, overt concern: a concern that leads to positive action. But action is impossible without
hope. We speak, perhaps imprecisely, about "being zealous for our
own salvation." What we really mean is that we have a lively hope
of our own salvation. As noted earlier, you will not and can not do
anything to reach a goal if you have no hope of reaching that goal.
And conversely, the brighter your hope the more you can and will do
to bring it to fulfillment. Hope, you see, is the key. It is the basis of
any and all your "zeal for your own salvation." Hope is at the
bottom of whatever zeal you have for your own welfare.

Just as surely, the key to your pastoral zeal for the welfare of
your people is the extent and the intensity of your hope that *they*
are going to heaven. If you do not have this hope that the Church
is on its way to the Father you cannot be a zealous priest. Action
is impossible without hope. You will not and in fact can not do
anything for your people's salvation except you be moved by a

living hope of their salvation. On the other hand, the more dynamic your Christian hope that this holy people of God is on its way to heaven, the more you can and will do to get them safely there. If only you see your people the Church as the Body of Christ en route back to the Father you will be a zealous priest. You cannot be otherwise. "Blessed be God . . . who makes hope live in us"!

9. "May your lives be rooted in love"—Priestly Charity

FAITH WITHOUT WORKS may be dead, but hope without works is sheer illusion. Pope Innocent XII said it is temerarious to detach hope from charity, but it is deadly to detach charity from hope. Christian hope has a postscript attached which it is fatal to overlook. There is no religious quietism more fraught with peril than that which would view Christian hope as a complacent, becalming inner glow whispering: "You are saved—take it easy." It is of the very essence of hope to be the spur to action. It belongs to hope to be the mother of good works. Any hope that would stifle good works is not hope at all. Your hope of heaven is not an absolute hope, it is a conditional hope. Charity, *agape,* the active love of God and neighbor, is an absolutely necessary condition to any hope of heaven you may have. You have no grounds whatsoever for expecting eternal happiness unless you love God and man. And is not this exactly what you were told that day you first made application for Christian hope? At your baptism you were asked what it was you sought there. You answered "Everlasting life." Do you remember what you were told? Notice the "if." Notice the condition. "If it is life you wish to enter, keep the commandments: love the Lord your

God with your whole heart and with your whole soul and with your whole mind, and love your neighbor as yourself." At the very outset you were clearly warned that for hope to be genuine it must be informed by charity. Only charity gives meaning and substance to hope.

And so, Father, Christian hope looks to the future only because it is deeply embroiled in the present. Hope focuses on the world above only because it rolls up its sleeves and throws itself into this world below. Hope propels you toward the City of God only because it bogs you down in the city of man.

The changeless truth is this: "I am the way . . . Nobody can come to the Father except through me" (John 14:6). And who is "me?" "Saul, Saul, why do your persecute me? . . . I was hungry and you gave me to eat . . ." Just as God came to man through man, so man comes to God only through man. "Nobody can come to the Father except through me. Through me as I exist *now:* in my Body made up of men who are the Church. It is only through me-them that anybody can come to the Father. It is only by active love for me-them that anybody can come to the Father. It is only by charity that any man gains everlasting life. It is only by charity that any Christian fulfils his hope."

Charity is a *theological* virtue. Its proper object is God. Charity above all else means love of God. In fact it means this exclusively. We tack the love of neighbor onto it only because the two are inseparable and, in the practical order, turn out to be one and the same thing.

You must love God. And while God has not been very explicit as to *how* you are to love him, he has been unmistakably explicit as to *how much.* You have got to love him with your whole heart and with your whole soul and with your whole mind and with your whole strength. He allowed no margin for error. He "threw the book" at you. You have got to love him completely and totally.

What uneasiness this "first and greatest commandment" causes us. We cannot deny it or pare it down. It is there, black on white, spelled out. The conflict between what we know we should do and what we know we do vis-a-vis this first and greatest commandment is perhaps THE problem of the spiritual life. It seems most acute in those truly conscientious persons who take this obligation most seriously: the Christian mother who confides in you that she is a hypocrite because, well really, she just does not love God more than she loves her children; the sincere priest (perhaps he is you) who winces at hearing himself say in prayer that he loves God above all things for what he is in himself. There is no need to labor the point. You know the problem—not only as it affects others but first-hand, as it affects you.

The clue to its solution, I think, lies in the fact that it is a *commandment*. It is not an evangelical counsel. Holy Scripture uses the very same word for this as for the decalogue. Because God gave it to us as a commandment properly so called, I think he tells us quite a lot about *how* we are to love him. Monsignor Ronald Knox furnished us this most welcome insight in one of his retreat conferences (*cfr. A Retreat for Lay People* (New York: Sheed and Ward), 1955, chapter seven).

God *commands* you to love him. This is highly significant. Can you imagine a situation in which you might *command* someone to love another? Take that good Catholic family down the street from the parish rectory: the parents would never command their mean little boy Johnny to love his old-maid Aunt Susie who is due in their home for a visit. They might give Johnny strict orders to be nice to the old girl, to open the door for her, to kiss her goodnight, to thank her for her present. All this they might command Johnny *to* do because all this they know Johnny *can* do. But command the little fellow to *love* Aunt Susie? Not on your life! They know nothing is more pointless: either Johnny will love Aunt Susie of his own accord without their telling him, or he will not love her and no amount to telling him will do any good. For, you see, what Aunt

Susie wants is Johnny's *affection*. And neither Johnny nor anyone pumps up affection at will. It either happens or it does not. The very word "affection" is revealing: something that affects you, something that happens to you, you do not cause it to happen. As Monsignor Knox observed, our English language in a rare burst of accuracy thus speaks of "falling in love." You have no real and true control over it. You can perhaps cause it *not* to happen, but you cannot cause it *to* happen.

Obviously, then, God could not command of you something over which you have no real and true control. Obviously, this first and greatest commandment has nothing at all to do with "affective" or spontaneous love. Obviously, spontaneous love is exactly that: it is beyond the pale of any order or injunction or command. What the first and greatest commandment does enjoin is "effective" or *deliberate* love of God. The trouble with us is that we do not distinguish between the two. We insist on confusing deliberate love with spontaneous love—with the kind of love that happens with no thanks to ourselves and announces its presence so forcefully in our feelings and emotions. Deliberate love has nothing to do with feelings or emotions. It resides in the *will*. Not only does it not occur spontaneously, *it has to be deliberately induced and cultivated.* You do not "fall into" it. You have to work at it. True, the *other* kind of love, spontaneous love, has so captured our fancy (as evidenced in our poetry and song) that we automatically equate it with the word "love" and tend to regard this as the only kind of love. But do not sell deliberate love short. It is by no means unknown or even uncommon among us. It is safe to say that most marriages after five years exist on deliberate love rather than on spontaneous love. Deliberate love is quite common in those families where one or the other parent finds that he can love one or the other child only by conscious effort. Most pastors, by the way, love their people by deliberate love rather than by spontaneous love!

What God commands of you, then, is a deliberate, cultivated love which resides in your will and ignores your feelings. That God may now and then give you one touch of spontaneous love, so that you feel you have actually "fallen in love" with God, is quite wonderful but also quite beside the point. What counts is the orientation of *your will:* whether you truly want and truly wish to love God. We have got to see that in the case of deliberate love to *want* to love God *is* to love God, to *will* to love God *is* to love God. So for you and me, Father, the pertinent question is not, "Do I love God with my whole heart and mind and strength?" It is rather, "Do I *want* to love God with my whole heart and mind and strength?" For you and me the *fair* question is not, "Do I love God above all things for his own sake?" but rather, "Do I honestly *will* to love God above all things for his own sake?" Of course, this must be a bona fide want. It must be an authentic act of the will and not a mere velleity. Our Lord went straight to the heart of the matter when he said, "If you love me, keep my commandments" (John 14:15). He could just as well have said, "If you keep my commandments you love me."

There is a deeper truth here which should not escape your notice: the virtue of charity is from God. You *can* love God only because God gives you the power to love him. However you love God, whether it be by spontaneous or by deliberate love, the power and the act of loving is from God himself. To deny this is to deny grace. Now God could just as well have given you a spontaneous love as a deliberate love. Why then did he choose the latter? Obviously because he prefers that we love him by a deliberate rather than a spontaneous love. But why? We do not know, but we might guess that it is because in some mysterious way he wanted us to MERIT eternal happiness. Now there is patently no "merit" in spontaneous love. What could be more pointless than a girl thanking a boy for having fallen in love with her? After all, it was spontaneous. The young man was not responsible for it. He did not make it happen— it just happened.

But there is "merit" in deliberate love—at least in our human way of looking at it. In this case you do have to *will* your love and you have to cultivate it—and occasionally in the face of considerable difficulty. Of course in speaking of the love of God, the doctrine of grace implies that in this case even the will to work at it comes from God. And so I can suggest no more than that in his own mysterious way God wants you to "merit" eternal happiness. Let us say that God prefers and therefore gives us a deliberate love of him rather than a spontaneous love, because he wants it to appear that we are responsible for loving him and therefore in some way responsible for meriting eternal happiness.

"This is the first commandment. And the second is like it: 'Thou shalt love thy neighbor as thyself'" (Mark 12:31). You will note not only that this too is a commandment strictly so called, but that it is a commandment specifically "like" the other. So here too the love that is enjoined is not a spontaneous love but a deliberate love. How many vexing problems in the spiritual life we and our people could avoid did we but keep this subtle distinction in mind. Loving your neighbor is the same thing as *wanting* to love him. It is the kind of love the poor troubled fellow has who tells you, "I can't stand the man I have to work with, but I am trying to think more charitably of him"—perhaps he is a priest, talking about his pastor or about his assistant. It is the kind of love the anxious penitent has who tells you, "I despise my meddling so-and-so of a mother-in-law, but I am trying not to show it and I do ask the Lord to help me feel differently toward her." What is in the feelings, in the emotions, in the reflexes, is unimportant. What is important is what is in the *will*, in the *intention*.

You are commanded to love your neighbor "as you love yourself." Well, how do you love yourself? Is it a love that is blind to your faults? If you are like me the answer is "Usually, yes." But then not always. How about your confession in the sacrament of penance? At that particular moment you are rather keenly aware of your faults. And do you not bow your head every Sunday in the presence of all your people and tell them in a voice loud and clear: "I have sinned very much in thought, word and deed, through my own fault, through my own most grievous fault?" There is quite a lot about yourself you do not love at all; in fact, you use such words as "detest, despise, hate." Therefore to love your neighbor as yourself does not mean to be blind to his faults either. Indeed you are to detest and hate his faults too. You are not to approve, overtly or by silence, the injustice, dishonesty, ungodliness or lustfulness you see in others. You do not love these in yourself, and so you are not to love them in others. You are to be as intolerant of their wickedness as you are of your own. But remember this: you are to hate evil in others for the same reason that you hate it in yourself. And why do you hate it in yourself? Because you love God? Well, yes; but mostly because you love yourself. You are appalled that someone you love so much should be guilty of this! Not only do you go right on loving yourself despite your wickedness, but the reason why you despise your wickedness is precisely that you do love yourself. This should also be the reason why you despise the wickedness you see in your neighbor.

All of this suggests the old axiom: "Hate the sin but love the sinner." Do you say there is more poetry than truth here? Do you say that it sounds great but that it is a pointless splitting of hairs? Do you ask how you can hate the evil a bad man does, without hating the bad man who does it? Do you ask how you can "hate the sin but love the sinner?" Well, Father, I do not know how you can. But I do know one thing: you do. There is one person to whom you consistently and effortlessly apply that debunked old axiom of hating the sin but loving the sinner. Of course, you are that man!

Have you ever noticed how our modern Catholic piety seems obsessed with non-charity rather than with charity? Avoiding uncharitableness preoccupies us much more than being charitable. How minutely we examine our consciences on our uncharitable acts. Yet we scarcely give one passing thought to the charitable acts we should have done. Nowhere is this more obvious than in the sacrament of penance.

Our Catholic people have an almost exclusively negative outlook on the law of fraternal charity. This is surpassing strange. After all, it is the law of fraternal charity and not the law against fraternal uncharity. After all, Jesus did say "love thy neighbor." He did not say "do not harm thy neighbor." And did not St. James warn us: "If a man has the power to do good, it is sinful in him to leave it undone" (James 4:17). And have you ever analyzed that famous passage on the general judgment in the twenty-fifth chapter of St. Matthew's gospel? It is just possible that all those condemned to hell had throughout their lives carefully avoided every uncharitable thought, word and deed. They are not judged at all for having been uncharitable. As far as we know, perhaps none of them ever was. They are condemned to hell not for having harmed their brethren, but they are condemned to hell for not having helped them. They are sentenced to eternal damnation not for having been uncharitable but for not having been charitable. There is a difference. One might even say there is a hell of a difference! Sitting back and scrupulously avoiding uncharitable acts can send a man straight to hell. What is commanded of us is that we go out in overt, positive charity to our fellow man.

Christian charity is not a negative entity. Christian charity is positive. This is the overwhelming testimony of Holy Scripture. This is THE lesson of the life of Jesus—a life which later could be summarized by his apostle Peter in the simple statement: "he went about doing good" (Acts 10:37). This is implicit in the fact that your love of neighbor is deliberate love rather than spontaneous love. Deliberate love resides in the will—and the only way you can be sure that kind is really there is to see it expressed in positive, overt action. Since you cannot *feel* deliberate love, you have to *see* it. Your mind can so easily play tricks on you. It is so easy for you to *think* that you love your neighbor. Actions speak louder than words or pious thoughts. Indeed, by their fruits you shall know them. "My children," said St. John, "let us show our love by the true test of action, not by taking phrases on our lips" (I John 3:18).

"Let us show our love by the true test of action." There is no other test—either of love or of faith or of hope. We have so conceptualized and so trichotomized the "three theological virtues" that it is difficult for us to see this. We love to savor each of the three separately and we have made each quite distinct from the other. This has not been good for us. And let me admit openly to a deep uneasiness over devoting separate conferences to faith, hope and charity in this retreat: I am afraid that I have thereby aided and abetted the perpetuation of this trichotomy. The Christian life is a response to God and the "three theological virtues" are that response. All three are the one, single response. All three are the one, indivisible yes-saying of the Christian who is the "I" to God who is the "Thou." All three are the one corporate response of the Church to her one Spouse, the Lord Jesus Christ.

All those neat distinctions of ours about sins which destroy charity but not faith or hope are really misleading. *Every* no-saying by any one of us, whatever its specific malice, strikes at all three theological virtues. You are not really capable of any sin which affects only charity in you but leaves faith and hope untouched. And conversely, you are not truly capable of any good work which "increases" only your charity without also affecting your faith and your hope. In your intellect you can perhaps distinguish between the "making" of an Act of Charity and the "making" of Acts of Faith and Hope—but in the order of concrete reality you cannot divorce an *act* of charity from either faith or hope.

Feodor Dostoievsky grasped this with keen insight. In a touching episode in *The Brothers Karamazov* he relates the visit of a "sentimental society lady" to the holy monk, Zossima. This good woman sought out Father Zossima because she was suffering intensely from "lack of faith." She pleaded for some assurance, for some proof. This wise and holy old man answered, "You cannot prove the faith, but you can be convinced of it." "How?" "By the experience of *active* love. Strive to love your neighbor actively and indefatigably. In as far as you advance in love you will grow surer of the reality of God . . . If you attain to perfect self-forgetfulness in the love of your neighbor, then you will believe without doubt, and no doubt can possibly enter your soul. This has been tried. This is certain." (*The Brothers Karamazov* (New York: Modern Library), p. 55). Nowhere have I seen a more eloquent—or more simple—statement that action is the true test and that to be charitable is to believe.

It was not until the end of his life that Jesus gave the specifically Christian turn to the law of fraternal charity. Now it is not just "love your neighbor as you love yourself." Now there is a new criterion: "You are to love one another as I have loved you" (John 15:12). This he promulgates not only as a "new" commandment, he singles it out as uniquely and specifically "his"—"This is *my* commandment." This is the infallible sign by which you can be recognized as belonging to him: "The mark by which all men will know you for my disciples will be the love you bear one another" (John 13:35). He first told us "You are to love one another as I have loved you," and the very next day he proceeded rather graphically to show us what he meant: he went out and died on a cross for us. Scarcely had he finished telling us "This is my commandment, that you are to love one another as I have loved you," when he added "Greater love than this no man has than that he lay down his life for his friends" (John 15:13). As he revealed it to us, *his kind* of love is not content merely to be the kind that is expressed in positive, overt charity. We do not see the true charity of Christ if we remember merely that "He went about doing good." His kind of love is the kind that is ready to die for his brothers.

Perhaps it is not entirely without significance that what he called "his commandment" he reserved for promulgation to his priests,

since it was not until the Last Supper that he gave it. This was the
theme of his ordination homily to his priests. It is primarily we
priests who should exemplify and fulfil *his* commandment to love
as he loved. As we shall see, the raison d'etre of our priesthood is
a positive, active, pastoral love of our brothers. This is the basis and
reason for the existence of the diocesan priesthood. Positive love of
neighbor is the key to the spirituality of the diocesan priesthood.

It is also the key to *any* bona fide Christian spirituality. Love
of neighbor is indeed the *"unum necessarium"* in the Christian life.
Augustine was not resorting to oversimplification when he said,
"Love—and then do anything at all you please." Neither was Paul
when he wrote, "The man who loves his neighbor has done ALL
that the law demands" (Rom. 13:9). It was not without reason
that in that whole memorable passage on the general judgment in
the twenty-fifth chapter of St. Matthew's gospel our Lord not only
mentions love of neighbor as the criterion of salvation, but mentions
absolutely nothing else. Not justice or chastity or obedience or
humility or prayer or even love of God. Surely that was an over-
sight: not to mention love of God. No it was not. In the practical
order love of God *is* the love of neighbor. It was to show this that
Luke in his gospel juxtaposed the parable of the Good Samaritan
and the Martha-Mary episode. There is no other way to show your
love of God "by the true test of action" except by positive charity
toward your neighbor. These are not two commandments but one.
Jesus himself said so. In St. Mark's gospel when he answered the
scribe "This is the first commandment and the second is like it," he
added a comment. It is a most interesting comment. "There is," he
said, "no other commandment greater than these" (Mark 12:31).
At first this strikes you as bad grammar. You would have expected
him to say "There are no greater commandments than these." But
no. "There is no other commandment greater than these." And so
St. John stated flatly: "If a man boasts of loving God, while he hates
his own brother, he is a liar . . . The man who loves God must be

one who loves his brother as well" (I John 4:20-21). In that same passage he says, "If we love one another, then we have God dwelling in us, and the love of God has reached its full growth in our lives" (I John 4:12). What an arresting statement! To love *one another* means that the love *of God* has reached full growth in us!

Father, you cannot separate Christ from the Church, for the Church is his own Body. This is why he was so insistent that you and I must love our brethren if we are to love him. During the intense cold of February, 1947, the Abbé Pierre, modern apostle of mercy to the poor of Paris, found a young father, mother and their little child homeless. He took them off the frozen streets of Paris and invited them to spend the night in his own poor little home. When they got there they found every room in the house already occupied by other homeless poor—except the room used as the chapel. The Abbé promptly moved the tabernacle into the unheated attic and put the young family in this room. When some of his associates professed shock at such irreverence to the Blessed Sacrament he replied, "Christ is not cold in the Blessed Sacrament, but he is cold in the body of a little child."

But there is a deeper reason why we Christians must love one another. In his body the Church, Christ lives, Christ works, Christ loves. The love you and I are to show, Father, is not merely to be *like* Christ's love—it *is* Christ's love! Because we who are the Church are the permanent incarnation of the Son of God, for us to love our brothers is Christ loving his brothers!

It was to priests to whom Jesus first said, "You are to love one another as I have loved you." And very shortly after he said it he went out and died on a cross. Every morning, Father, you and I hold that immolated body of his in our hands, and the blood he shed is there in the cup. Surely we, who are thus daily reminded of how he loves us, should find it easier than the rest to love one another as he loved us.

10. "God's loving design"—The Way

"How to Make $1,000,000 in the Stock Market." "How to Win Friends and Influence People." "How to" books have always been popular. In Chicago's O'Hare airport I noticed one entire book rack labeled simply "HOW TO." Treatises on how to do it exist on almost every conceivable subject. Religion is no exception. Certainly our religion is no exception. Down through the centuries wise and holy and sometimes foolish men, in response to popular demand, have supplied us with systems on how to live the Christian life. The Church has repudiated some of these systems and given her blessing to others. But as far as I know the Church has given official, liturgical status only to one. And that one is the first one, the original one given us in the New Testament, the one St. Paul calls "God's loving design" (Eph. 1:9).

Father, whether we like it or not we are masters in the Christian life. As "God's men" it is our office to point the way to him to others and, of course, it is properly assumed that we know the way ourselves. We secular priests can be forgiven for not being experts in teaching the ascetical systems of Francis de Sales or of Father Olier or of the Sodality. But we can not be forgiven for not being experts in teaching God's plan; for while we may not be de Sales men or Sodality men we are, all of us, God's men.

God's plan, simply put, is this: to return mankind to himself, through his Son Jesus Christ, in the Holy Spirit. The formula is more simple still: from, through, in, to—*a, per, in, ad*. *A Patre, per Filium, in Spiritu, ad Patrem.*

Now this should have a familiar ring to it. The Pauline epistles are shot through with it. *"A, per, in, ad"*—these four little words are the key to a plan, to a secret. They are the key to God's own plan for returning mankind to himself. They are the key to what Paul calls "God's merciful design" or "God's loving design." This divine plan is none other than "the mystery," "the secret" about which Paul spoke so often and of which he proclaimed himself the herald. In Romans he called it "the mystery hidden from us through countless ages, but now made plain." In Colossians he said of it, "This was the secret that had been hidden from all the ages and generations of the past; now God has revealed it to us." And in Ephesians he said, "I publish to the world the plan of this mystery, kept hidden from the beginning of time in the all-creative mind of God. The principalities and powers of heaven are to see, now, made manifest in the Church, the subtlety of God's wisdom. Such is his eternal purpose, centered in Christ Jesus."

The proclamation of this secret *is* the gospel. The good news is precisely this: the announcement of "God's eternal purpose, centered in Christ Jesus." In heralding it the articulate Paul soared to his highest eloquence. Let me quote only two of the more memorable passages and, as you listen, note the recurring *"a, per, in, ad."*

In Ephesians, chapter two: "For through (Jesus Christ) we have access in one Spirit to the Father." And also in Ephesians this—by all odds one of the most amazing and inspiring passages in all of Scripture: "Blessed be God! . . . He has chosen us out, in Christ, to be saints . . . marking us out by the decree of his will to be his adopted children through Jesus Christ. Thus he would manifest the splendor of that grace by which he has taken us into his favor in the person of his beloved Son. It is in him and through his blood

that we enjoy redemption . . . So rich is God's grace! This was his
loving design, centered in Christ: to give history its fulfilment by
resuming everything in him; all that is in heaven, all that is on
earth, summed up in him. In him it was our lot to be called, singled
out beforehand to suit his purpose . . . In him you too were called
. . . In him you too learned to believe, and had the seal set on your
faith by the promised gift of the Holy Spirit: a pledge of the
inheritance which is ours, to redeem it for us and bring us into
possession of it and so to manifest God's glory" (Eph. 1:3–14).

Father, we have heard about "the secret of the Little Flower" but
this is God's secret. We have heard about de Montfort's way, but
this is God's way. I am not suggesting that these other ways or
systems of the Christian life are unworthy of our attention, but
I am saying that this one *demands* our attention. As God's men
we must be experts at it; not merely because we are charged with
guiding others by it, but most especially because we must follow it
ourselves. Because we are uniquely God's men, we must personally
take up God's way. We, even more than those we lead, must pattern
our spirituality after *his* formula for the Christian life: to the
Father, through Jesus Christ, in the Holy Spirit. We who teach
others about the Blessed Trinity must teach them not only that it is
a truth to which our minds assent; above all we must teach them by
our example that the Blessed Trinity is a way of life to be lived.
We must teach them that it is, in fact, the authentic Christian way
of life: *ad Patrem, per Filium, in Spiritu.*

AD PATREM. God the Father must be not only the ultimate
goal of our existence but also the immediate object of our piety.
Well, is He?

Yes and no. Vis-à-vis God the Father, we priests are split per-
sonalities. We pray one way in our official piety, another in our
personal piety. As *priests,* in our official role, our prayer *is* directed
to the Father. As *men,* in our strictly personal prayer, we scarcely
give God the Father a passing thought.

In our sacerdotal, liturgical prayer-life we do go to the Father. Our priestly prayer is *"ad Patrem."* The Mass affords the perfect example, for nowhere are we more "officially" priests than at the altar of sacrifice. What do we do at Mass? We direct our worship wholly and entirely *"ad Patrem."* We introduce each of the three so-called principal parts of the Mass with an explicit invocation of God the Father. We begin the Offertory by saying "Receive, O holy Father, almighty and eternal God, this spotless host . . ." The Canon's opening words are *"Te igitur, clementissime Pater . . ."* We introduce the Communion service of the Mass by addressing "Our Father who art in heaven . . ." And it is to God the Father we direct our thanksgiving in the Preface: "It is indeed fitting and right, it is our duty, it is our salvation, to thank You, Lord, holy Father, almighty and everlasting God, always and everywhere . . ." Nor should it escape our notice that even the words of Consecration are addressed to the Father. These hallowed words are not a disembodied quote; we direct them to the Father. The *Qui Pridie,* which is the immediate context of the consecration narrative, is addressed *"ad Deum Patrem."* And while it is the passion, resurrection and ascension of the *Son* we recall to mind at the *Unde et memores,* it is to the *Father* we direct this remembrance. And of course, it is to the Father we offer the holy and stainless Victim in the *"offerimus"* portion of that prayer. Nor should the community prayers of the Mass (Collect, Secret and Post-communion) be overlooked. Of approximately fourteen hundred in the Roman Missal, some twelve hundred are directed *to* the Father, *through* the Son, *in* the Holy Spirit. We note too that the few which are not directed to the Father are comparatively recent arrivals in the Missal and that none at all is directed to the Blessed Mother or to the Saints. From beginning to end, the Mass we celebrate is unmistakably *"ad Patrem."* In our official role as priests, our piety is without doubt "to the Father."

But once we step down from the altar, what a change! How

seldom in our own private prayer do we turn person-to-Person to this wondrous Father whose sons we are. Apart from the Lord's Prayer, do you ever in your personal prayer-life really address the First Person of the Blessed Trinity? Does God the Father exist as a real, living Person for you in your personal piety?

We priests humbly exult in the title "other Christs." We are undeniably "other Christs" in our official sacerdotal acts. But we must be "other Christs" in our personal piety too. Ours must be like His. Well, Christ's personal piety was essentially *filial*. His own private devotion was unexceptionally to the Father. The gospels are athrob with the record of Jesus' deep, real, living devotion to the Father. He oriented everything toward Him. He lived only for the Father. He came for nothing else than to do the Father's will. All the glory is the Father's. The only prayer he taught us was a prayer to the Father. All that he was, all that he had he devoted completely to the Father. The night before he died he revealed that his mission essentially was to glorify his Father on earth: "Father, I have glorified Thee on earth; I have finished the work you gave me to do" (John 17:4).

And with what urgency he sought to teach us that this Father loves us too: "The Father himself loveth you because you have loved me and have believed that I came forth from God" (John 16:27). He assured us that the Father not only loves us but actually comes to us and makes His continual abode with us (John 14:23). He said very plainly that this Father is not only *his* but *ours* also, for after his resurrection he appeared to Mary Magdalen and said, "Go to my brethren and say to them, I ascend to my Father and to your Father." (John 20:17) Jesus called us his "brethren" or "brothers" not merely because he shared our human nature; by what he said to the Magdalen he left no doubt about why and how we are his brothers: he and we have the same Father!

As God's men it is our office boldly to defend the rights of God. Our office is religion, and religion means giving God what is due

Him, it means giving God his rights. Among the first of these is his strict right to the worship-of-Him-as-Father by all of us whom He adopted as his sons in Baptism. You and I can hardly defend this primary right unless first we observe it ourselves: in our *personal* piety as well as in our priestly acts. The Christian religion at its deepest point is this Father-son relationship. Any genuinely Christian spirituality must be founded on this relationship. We may use and promote other ways of the spiritual life—but always and only within the framework of *this* way, for this way is God's way. Whatever else it might be, a spirituality which is not ultimately directed "*ad Patrem*" is not authentic Christian spirituality. To be Christian it must be filial.

Ad Patrem—PER FILIUM. "I am the way . . . no man comes to the Father except through me" (John 14:6). "*Te igitur, clementissime Pater, per dominum nostrum Jesum Christum filium tuum . . .*" (Canon of the Mass). Jesus Christ is the way to the Father. He is, in fact, the *only* way to the Father and there is no other: "I am the way . . . No man comes to the father except through me" (John 14:6). Therefore Jesus Christ has to be known first. To know where you are going you have first got to know the way there. "Where I go you know, and the way you know . . . Then Thomas said, 'Lord, we do not know where you are going and how can we know the way there?' And Jesus said, 'I am the way'" (John 14:4-6). And so Christian spirituality is centered in Jesus Christ, and nowhere is this more evident than in the sacred liturgy. ". . . such is God's eternal purpose, centered in Christ Jesus" (Eph. 3:11).

That the way is *to* the Father through the Son is constitutional to "God's loving design." To hold that it is *to* the Son is unconstitutional. It is not *to* the Son but *through* the Son. This is more than a semantic nicety. It is a truth of the first magnitude in the Christian life. But we tend to confuse it—we keep getting our prepositions mixed up. We keep wanting to make it *to* the Son rather than *through* the Son.

We have got to realize that the Christian way of life is not *to* Christ, but *through* Christ to the Father. Authentic Christian prayer is not so much prayer *to* Christ as it is prayer through and with Christ to the Father. True Christian worship is not so much the worship of *Christ* as it is worship of the *Father* made through Christ and in his Spirit.

This is in no wise to say or even to imply that Jesus Christ is not God. He is God, and therefore He is not only worthy of adoration but *inescapably* worthy of adoration. By all means let us keep and promote all those authentic Catholic devotions whose purpose is to give adoration to God the Son. But let us not ignore the lesson in Christian prayer given us by the Church in her liturgy: the sacred liturgy's way is through Christ to the Father. *Lex orandi est lex credendi.* In fact, let us not ignore the lesson given us by our Lord Himself in his own life. Did God the Son become incarnate among us in order to get us to adore him? Did he not in fact come among us precisely and obviously as man, as one of us, and definitely not as Lord-God? Did not St. Paul assure us that his incarnation was essentially a "*kenosis,*" an emptying-out of his Godly glory? This man was exactly like any other man, and because he was, he was tested in every way like any other man "only without sin" (Heb. 14:15).

We find it difficult really to come to terms with the truth that the Word was made *flesh*. We meditate lovingly on the Godness implied in that equation but we shy away from the humanness implied in it. Jesus Christ is one of us; he is true man. In his life he went to great lengths to get us to see and accept this. He allowed only the chosen three to see him on Tabor, but he hung there on another hill in a pitiably human state for *all* to see. And while he did give abundant evidence that he possessed an immediate consciousness of himself as Son of God, every one of his own references to his divinity is strangely veiled. But how unabashedly forthright he was about being man. He never once taught us or counseled us to pray to him, but he did ask us to pray in his name to the Father. The one prayer he himself taught us is a prayer to the Father . . . He was and he is the God-man.

Ever since his resurrection he is indeed and obviously the *"Kyrios,"* the Lord—but significantly *our* Lord, Dominus *noster.* One of *us* is exalted in Godly glory at the Father's right hand! If it be wrong to ignore that he is God, it is equally wrong to ignore that he is man. Yet in practice this is what we today often do. To modern Catholics Jesus Christ is God, and God is Jesus Christ, period. So vigorous was Christendom's rejection of the Arian heresy that in the process we have all but forgotten that Jesus Christ is also and indeed *true man.* Even in his glory as *Kyrios*-God he remains forever one of us. So singlemindedly did we defend the truth against the Arians that Jesus Christ is true God, that we lost touch somehow with the rest of the truth about him: that he is one of us. Little wonder that the doctrine of the Mystical Body went into eclipse for centuries, for the Church is the Body of Christ and the only body he has is a *human* body. And so we Christians lost our sense of solidarity with Jesus Christ our Head. We lost that sense of vital contact with him as our Elder Brother, as the first-born of the new creation. Gradually we came to regard him, simply and exclusively, as God.

While there is nothing wrong about this, there is something disjunctive about it. He became for us a loving and tenderly merciful God, to be sure—but also remote and quite apart, as the infinite God must be remote and apart from finite, sinful men. And so we began adoring the Blessed Sacrament (whereas before the emphasis had been on uniting with It). And we inserted numerous genuflections and an elevation into the Mass. And we began writing Collects for the Mass addressed to the Lord-God Jesus Christ. And we began making his brethren, the Christian people, kneel at Mass, kneel interminably, thereby helping them forget that they were at Mass to worship their Father as sons in union with THE Son.

Slaves kneel; true sons do not. How futile to remind the Christian people (as they had once been reminded): "God sent his own Son, born of a woman . . . to make us sons by adoption . . . No longer then are you a slave, you are a son" (Gal. 4:4-7). Now of course there was absolutely nothing wrong in this development: it is every bit as orthodox to worship God the Son as it is to worship God the Father. But it did become complicated and confusing. It became particularly confusing in the Mass. Were we there to worship the Father or to worship the Son? Is the Christian way *ad Patrem per Filium,* or is it simply *ad Filium?*

We have got to bring "God's holy people" back onto track. For they are not only his holy people, they are also his bewildered people. We have got to get them to see that the Christian way is *ad Patrem per Filium.* We have the means by which to get them to see this—and that means is the Mass. The Christian way reaches its finest hour in the Mass. One of our major objectives must be to teach them to see that the Mass is worship of that real Person, God the Father; and that it is worship which we make not only through our Head and Brother, Jesus Christ, but also with him and in him. *"Per ipsum et cum ipso et in ipso . . . est Tibi, Deo Patri."* And the best and possibly only way of teaching them to *see* this is to make it possible for them to *experience* it—every Sunday at Mass. We and they must grasp the simple meaning of those simple words: "I am the way . . . no one comes to the Father except through me" (John 14:6). We and they are Christians, and to be a Christian is to be with the Son and in the Son. How relentlessly Paul uses those two extraordinary expressions: *in* Christ, *with* Christ. We who have been baptized have been "taken up into Christ" (Rom. 6:3). We are the body of Jesus Christ, the Son. In a sense we *are* the Son. Augustine, that daring theologian, did not hesitate to say: "The children of God are the body of the only Son of God, and since he is the head and we are the members, there is but one Son of God. (*Epist. ad Parthos,* P. L. XXXV, 2055) Not only are we (by baptism) become Christians, we are become Christ. My brothers, wonder, rejoice: for we are made Christ! If he is the head and we the members, then together he and we are the whole Christ." (*In Joh.* 21, P. L. XXXV, 1568) How long since any of us has dared speak this boldly about our solidarity with Christ!

Father, one thing we must see: this *way*—this "with-Christness" en route to the Father—this is not just a dogma or an abstract truth. It is an *activity*. It is a dynamism. Therefore you cannot "know" this merely by your intellect. Really to know it you must *experience* it. Knowledge here cannot be merely conceptual, it has to be experiential. What a challenge this presents to you and me! We can never "teach" our people about this merely by telling them about it. It is in the experiential situation of the parish Sunday Mass that we will "teach" them this—we have got to get them to feel it, to sense it, to experience it. For them really to know what Jesus meant when he said "I came forth from the Father . . . and I am on my way back to the Father" (John 16:28), both they and we have got to experience *this:* "I came forth from the Father, and now I, the *whole* Christ, head and members, am on my way back to the Father." This is the way—God's way.

But there is more to it. Not only is it *ad Patrem per Filium,* but *ad Patrem per Filium IN SPIRITU.* The way is "in the Holy Spirit."

Canon Masure in the twilight of his life, reviewing the great breakthroughs in Christology and Ecclesiology achieved during his lifetime, indulged in the luxury of a prediction: the prediction that the next significant breakthrough, the next great insight, would center in the Holy Spirit. Maybe. Maybe not. Maybe his role is to remain hidden, to remain out of the spotlight himself so that he can the better reveal to us the Father and the Son. This after all is his role, for this is the prayer we sing to him at Pentecost: *"Per Te sciamus da Patrem, noscamusque Filium*—Through You may we come to know the Father and to recognize the Son" (Pentecost hymn, Roman Breviary).

But certainly any "knowing better" of the Father and the Son means also to know him better. In the Self-giving of God "*ad intra*" which is the Blessed Trinity, the Holy Spirit is the term. He completes and closes out this Self-giving. He is the Omega of God's internal Self-giving.

But in the Self-giving of God "ad extra" which is the Church, the Holy Spirit is the starting point, the point of entry. He is the Alpha of God's external Self-giving. As Paul puts it: "In one Spirit were we all baptized into one Body" (I Cor. 12:13). And we note that it is of water *and* the Holy Spirit that a man is *born* again. The Spirit who is in the Son bursts forth from Christ by virtue of his resurrection, takes hold of us and incorporates us into the risen Christ to make us "sons in the Son." Joined to Christ by the Spirit, we go *in* the Spirit *through* Christ *to* the Father. "Through Christ we have access in one Spirit to the Father" (Eph. 2:18). But it is he, none other than the Holy Spirit, who is our point of entry. In the Self-giving of God "ad extra" which is the Christian mystery, it is the Holy Spirit who comes to us as the *first* Gift. "Those who follow the leading of God's Spirit are all God's sons; the Spirit you have received is not as of old a spirit of slavery to govern you by fear. It is the Spirit of adoption which makes us cry out 'Abba, Father'" (Rom. 8:14-15).

Yes, the Holy Spirit dwells within us as the first principle of our return to the Father. But this is an *active* indwelling: he dwells within us as the source and principle of our prayer and worship. Christian prayer is prayer *in* the Spirit. "When we do not know what prayer to offer, to pray as we ought, the Spirit himself intercedes for us with groans beyond all utterance" (Rom. 8:26). Some of our difficulties with prayer might ease if we could stop being such rank Pelagians in our whole approach to prayer, and begin finding Faith to encounter the Holy Spirit who dwells within us as the source of prayer. It is those who follow the leading of God's Spirit who are God's sons. Christian prayer ultimately is always prayer in the Spirit, through the Son, to the Father. It must be because this is the Christian way. This is God's way. His own loving design: *in Spiritu, per Filium, ad Patrem.*

11. The Diocesan Priesthood:
Its Theology

WE DIOCESAN PRIESTS are unique: we are no longer laymen, we are not monks, we are not clerics regular. We are secular priests. The Church, in Canon 124, orders us to lead "holier" lives and to excel by the example of our virtue and our good works. All this is expected of us as pure matter of course. It is simply a *fiat* of Canon Law. Yet we have never been told HOW. There is not now, nor has there ever been, an asceticism specifically for diocesan priests—one tailored to *our* needs, inspired by *our* ideals. There is much ado in the Church today over development of a spirituality for the laity. This is a providential movement, long overdue. While it is true that there is only one Christian spirituality and not many, the approaches to it may vary. The holy people of God are neither clerics nor monks. For too long we have tried to foist a monkish or clerical spirituality on them, with both the ideals and the means inspired by non-lay spirituality, and with all their books on marriage written by celibates. Yes, it is time we looked into the theological bases of a bona fide lay approach to Christian spirituality. But an approach to Christian spirituality proper to us diocesan priests is just as long overdue and, unfortunately in this case, not much is being done about it.

Look at the record. The asceticism under which we diocesan priests try to live is a legacy bequeathed us by monasticism and, more latterly, by clerics regular. Celibacy we got from the Fathers of the desert and early monasticism. The Divine Office we got from the Benedictines and the mendicant friars. The daily rosary we got from the Dominicans. Methodical meditation and the daily examen and the annual retreat we got from the Jesuits. The daily visit to the Blessed Sacrament we got from the Redemptorists. While gratefully acknowledging our debt, we do ask to be heard. The asceticism handed us is neither *from* us nor *by* us nor, originally, even *for* us. It is at best a haphazard melange—a kind of mix-master ascetical hodge-podge. Dare we say we deserve better? Are we diocesan priests either impertinent or impudent in asking that just for once *we* be taken into account in charting the spiritual blueprint by which we are to live the "holier" life expected of us?

As it is, conflict is the watchword of the asceticism under which we strive. The breviary, our minimum daily spiritual exercises, our priestly work, our needed leisure and recreation—all these are in conflict with one another and we are caught in the middle: confused, bewildered and discouraged. Why must there be conflict between the very elements whose purpose is to advance us in the spiritual life? We secular priests are in urgent need of a sensible synthesis under which we can lead the holy life that is demanded of us.

Don't be alarmed! I am not quite brash enough and not nearly learned enough to attempt sketching such a synthesis. But I do submit that if ever it is to be done we must begin at the beginning. Theology does have consequences. Bad theology has bad consequences and good theology sometimes has good consequences. Foundations *are* important. If we diocesan priests are ever to think through our own spirituality, we have got first to think through the nature and meaning of our own unique priestly office. We must begin with the theology of the diocesan priesthood. If we want ever to think right about our priestly *life*, we have got first to think right about our priest*hood*. The concept of a diocesan-priest spirituality depends on the concept of the diocesan priesthood.

We diocesan priests kid about our bishops—and at times some of us wax monumentally profane about them. But you and I cannot afford to forget one thing, Father: as diocesan priests we have relevance and meaning and existence only by and for and because of our bishop. With that said, and with a word of warning that the limitations of time impose the conscious risk of oversimplifying a very complex subject, let us begin at the beginning.

It is *de fida definita* that there is only one Priest (Denzinger, 122). He is Jesus Christ, true God and true man. Priest is *sacerdos*, "*sacra dans*": giving the All-holy God to the people and giving the holy people of God to God. Priest is *Pontifex*: builder of a two-way bridge between God and people. He is, in short, priest *because he is mediator:* uniting God with man in order to unite man with God. Jesus Christ is not only Priest, he is the only priest because he alone, in his Person, united divinity with humanity. He did this in the Incarnation by the hypostatic union. Jesus Christ is the only priest because he alone unites humanity with divinity: "nobody comes to the Father except through me." Jesus alone is priest by nature: he is that by his two-fold nature, divine and human. "For there is," said St. Paul, "only one God and only one mediator between God and men, himself man, Jesus Christ" (I Tim. 2:5).

Note that Jesus Christ *is* priest because he is the "one mediator between God and men." *Mediatorship* is the essential note in the definition of priesthood—offering sacrifice is not. I submit that our notion of priesthood today has been unduly influenced by the notion of sacrifice. True, Christ's supreme priestly act was his sacrifice on the cross. It was on Good Friday that Jesus was most magnificently priest. But that was not when he *became* priest, nor is that why he *was* priest. He became priest at the Incarnation. He was priest every moment of his life in everything he did and said. Granted, his supreme and decisive priestly act was the Cross; but it was not that that made him priest. You must not confuse the *office* of mediatorship with the *means of exercising* that mediatorship—not even with the supreme and decisive means of exercising it. Calvary was a sacrifice because Jesus was priest. Jesus was not priest because Calvary was a sacrifice. You must not equate the concept of priesthood with the concept of offering sacrifice. One is not a priest because he offers sacrifice: what he offers is a sacrifice because he is a priest. Mediatorship is the essential note in the definition of priesthood. You must never forget this, even while recognizing that this mediatorship realizes its fullest actuality in the act of offering sacrifice. Jesus alone is priest because he alone, in the Incarnation, united the divine with the human. He alone in his Person bridged the gulf between God and men. He alone is mediator who brought God to man and man to God. "I am the way . . . Nobody comes to the Father except through me." "God became man," said Augustine, "in order that man might become divine."

If Jesus Christ is the only Priest, it follows that no one else is priest in his own right. But does this mean that Jesus could not communicate his priesthood to others by participation? The problem has a parallel. It has an antecedent—and an antecedent solution. Just as Jesus Christ is the only priest, so too is he the only Son—the only Son of God. He alone enjoys this prerogative by nature. But "God's loving design" found a way to share this sonship: by adoption through grace, by participation in the divine nature. Baptism makes us sons of God—indeed not sons by nature as Christ is, but sons by adoption, by election, by participation. We become sons in the Son.

You and I would never have been called to divine sonship if

Jesus were not THE Son. But, granted that he is the Son, we can hope to become sons through him. As Matthias Scheeben puts it, ". . . if God demands of our faith the avowal that he is the Father of his only-begotten Son, he thereby wills us openly to profess and acknowledge that he is our Father too; if he demands that we believe in his Son, he wills also that we acknowledge ourselves to be his children" (*The Mysteries of Christianity* (St. Louis: Herder), 1947, p. 124). God has revealed himself not merely as Father but precisely as our Father because he wills us to become his sons in the Son. "God's loving design" found a way, and gave us a sacrament as the sign and means of sharing this sonship, and did so without prejudice to Christ's unique and monopolistic right to Sonship. This is the key. So too there would never have been any genuine priesthood in this world if Jesus had not been THE priest. But granted that he is the priest, we might hope to become priests through him by participation. Here too "God's loving design" found a way, and gave us a sacrament as the sign and means of sharing this priesthood, and did so without prejudice to Christ's unique and monopolistic right to Priesthood.

Mark here a primary truth about our priesthood: just as men are sons of God only by participation in the one Sonship and not by right or by nature, so too men are priests only by participation in the one Priesthood and not by right or by nature. Jesus himself inaugurated this participation in the persons of the Apostles. It is *de fide definita* that he did this at the Last Supper when he said to them: "*Hoc facite in meam commemorationem*" (Trent, Sess. XXII, Can. 2, Denzinger 949). It was then that his Priesthood took on the new dimension of priesthood-by-participation. It was then he, the only Priest, made his Apostles priests-by-participation. But when he did, he entrusted to them *all* his functions of mediatorship: teaching, preaching, rendering service, sanctifying, reconciling, offering sacrifice. We know this because he himself told them later: "As the Father sent me, so I now

send you out in turn" (John 20:21). The Apostles were "con-
formed" to Christ the Priest in *all* his ministerial functions. As
Priest, as the "one mediator" between his Father and men, Jesus
had prayed for men and in their name, he had taught them and
preached to them, he had ministered to them in untiring personal
service, he had sanctified them and forgiven their sins; he had
fed them when they were hungry, healed them when they were sick;
he had visited them, exhorted them, consoled them. He announced
the good news to them and laid the foundations of the Church. Especially did he offer a redeeming and at-one-ing sacrifice. Then he
personally delegated the Apostles to *all* these priestly functions: "as
the Father sent me, so I now send you out in turn." Now they
were priests, but not in their own right. They were priests only
by participation in his Priesthood. They were his "other selves":
the One Priest diffused, spread abroad and passed on. What's
more, they were to send out other "other selves" in turn until
the end of time. "And behold I am with you (as mediators sent
to teach, govern and sanctify) all through the days that are coming, until the consummation of the world" (Matt. 28:20).

It is imperative that we grasp the full significance of this; it
was *as apostles* Jesus made them priests. What a revolutionary
departure this was! Heretofore priests existed only to offer ritual
sacrifice. Priests were usually the most withdrawn and inaccessible
of men. They were not "sent out." They were "holy men" in
the etymological sense that they were set apart, physically set apart
from the people. More often than not the people in whose name
they offered sacrifice were not even allowed to be present when
they offered sacrifice. Until now priests were shut off, cloistered,
segregated from the people. But Jesus Christ the only true Priest,
by his own admission, came "not to be ministered unto but to
minister" (Mark 10:45). These priests of his remembered that he
had once told them: "You know that the rulers of the Gentiles
lord it over them . . . Not so is it among you. On the contrary,

whoever wishes to become great among you shall be your servant; and whoever wishes to be first among you shall be your slave" (Matt. 20:25–27). On the very night he shared his Priesthood with them he told them: "You call me Master and Lord, and you say well, for so I am. If, therefore, I the Lord and Master have washed your feet, you also ought to wash the feet of one another. For I have given you an example, that as I have done to you, so you also should do. Amen, amen, I say to you, no servant is greater than his master, nor is one who is sent greater than he who sent him" (John 13:13–16).

This was unheard-of talk from a priest! And he the only Priest! The same who said "I have compassion on the multitude." He the only Priest, priest by everything he was and said and did, changed the concept of priesthood. He was no segregated "holy man," set apart from sweating, sinning, suffering humanity. He did not merely offer sacrifice for men in some sealed-off temple holy of holies: he went out to them in untiring personal service. His proudest boast was: "I stand in the midst of you as one who serves"! (Luke 22:27). He, the only Priest, was the *servus servorum Dei!* And then he sent out apostles to do as he had done—after he had made them priests like himself. Priesthood is mediatorship. Mediating through offering sacrifice? Yes. But, as revealed to us by the only Priest, more than that: mediating also through personal service. *His* priesthood includes charity. It *is* charity. This was new, revolutionary. To participate in his priesthood means to participate in his charity—in his compassionate concern for and his personal service to those whom, as mediator, he would unite to God. Ever since, to be a priest means also to be an apostle: one who is sent to minister to people: to live among them, to mingle with them and be "in their midst," to work for them, to teach them, to lead them, to exhort, reprove, console, sanctify and reconcile them with God.

Now mark you well that it was *the apostles* who were ordained priests at the Last Supper. Implicit here is the simple but essential truth that the true sacramental priesthood, the complete and integral Christian priesthood, is that of the apostles and their successors, *not that of priests*. It was to the apostles Christ the only Priest communicated direct participation in his priesthood. Ever since the Last Supper even until now, it is to the successors of the apostles that Christ the only Priest communicates a direct participation in his priesthood. Your priesthood and mine, Father, the "presbyteral priesthood," is not at all a *direct* participation in the priesthood of Christ. It is a direct participation in the priesthood of an apostle-bishop and thus only indirectly, only through him, a participation in the priesthood of Christ. It is sobering for you and me to reflect, despite all the nice things said of us at our First Solemn Mass, that the kind of priesthood you and I share was not personally and directly instituted by our Lord. The "presbyterate" (your kind of priesthood and mine) derived directly not from Christ but from the apostles-bishops. Chronologically it even made its appearance after the diaconate, and with a less original aspect than the diaconate. Your kind of priesthood and mine, historically, is a child of necessity. It is the offspring of charity. The apostles-bishops could no longer personally cope with the demands of this new kind of priestly office, so first they shared part of it with the diaconate and, slightly later, a greater part of it with the presbyterate.

Theologically there is no problem here. He who is capable of communicating the whole, *a fortiori* is capable of communicating a part. He who can give all can certainly give some. Christ the only Priest, who "sent out" the apostles-bishops as full participants in his own priestly office, sent them out specifically as he had been sent: that is, with the same power of communicating to others this full participation. Obviously, if these apostles-bishops could communicate to others the full participation in Christ's priesthood, they could also communicate to still others a partial participation.

You and I are priests by such indirect and subordinate participation. If the bishop is priest only as a necessary "other self" of Christ the only Priest, you and I are priests only as necessary "other selves" of our bishop. That there is anything disillusioning or degrading to you and me implied here is too obviously false for comment. As a matter of fact, it is our glory—and specifically our glory as diocesan priests, as we shall see.

Let me pause here to recap these truths which must form the basis of a theology of the diocesan priesthood and, therefore, the basis of a spirituality for diocesan priests.

Jesus Christ, true God and true man, is the only Priest. He is sole Priest because he is sole Mediator: in the hypostatic union alone uniting God with man and man with God. As Cardinal Suhard put it: "It is not just that he *has* the priesthood, he *is* the priesthood. The Christian Priesthood is not some *thing,* it is Some *One.*" In the exercise of this priesthood he opened a new frontier in the concept and meaning of the office. It is founded on charity: on outgoing personal service to those who are to be united with God. *"Misereor super turbam."*

Just as Jesus Christ the only Son shared his Sonship with men, so did Jesus Christ the only Priest share his priesthood with men. He shares it directly and personally and fully with the apostles and their successors, the bishops. But it is *as apostles* that he shares his priesthood with them. The magnificent pattern of ministry and service which was so much a part of his priesthood, is an integral and essential note in their sharing in it. The primary characteristic of this priesthood, this mediatorship, is charity: to stand in the midst of men as one who serves.

These priests-by-participation, the apostles-bishops, were sent as he was sent: that is, with the power of sending others. And so throughout history they have communicated to other bishops this full and direct participation in the one priesthood of Jesus Christ— a priesthood characterized now not only by offering sacrifice, but also and essentially by dogged love of the brethren: "you must go out and compel them to come in" (Luke 14:23).

Very early the practical demands of this charity utterly overwhelmed them. So first they shared part of their responsibility with the diaconate and, not long after, a greater part of their responsibility and of their priestly powers with the presbyterate. This is the origin, the raison d'etre, the definition of the diocesan priesthood. It was the need of continuing this ministry of charity which brought us into being.

From this, two truths of the first magnitude for you and for me emerge. First, we diocesan priests exist only in relation to our bishop. In relation to Christ the Priest, yes; but dependent on and in collaboration with our bishop. This truth is even clearer in the case of auxiliary bishops, as noted in the distinction that they are auxiliaries to the bishop of a diocese and not auxiliary bishops of a diocese. We too, when all is said and done, are auxiliaries to our bishop. To this day the definition of a vocation to the priesthood is based on the actual existence of this need: it is precisely and only because a bishop *needs* helpers that he calls men to Holy Orders. If the bishop does not need them they have no vocation!

The second truth of immense consequence for you and me here is that we share in the *apostolate* of the bishop. If we share in his priesthood we also share in his apostolate, since in him the two are inseparable. In fact, this apostolate is *why* we share in his priesthood. But you and I are *diocesan* priests, and therefore our participation in the priesthood of the bishop is unique. All priests, diocesan and religious, share in the apostolate of an apostle-bishop. But let everyone recognize that we diocesan priests do so in a more direct, personal and permanent manner than religious-order priests. They too are "sent" to help an apostle-bishop in his apostolate. They too are his "auxiliaries." But we are more properly his auxiliaries. Our priesthood is more directly and more personally tied-in to the priesthood of the Episcopacy. It is we diocesan priests whom a successor of the apostles has personally called to shoulder and to share his own "daily burden: the anxious solicitude of all the churches" (II Cor. 11:28). Because we are the proper auxiliaries of an apostle-bishop, in a unique and proper sense our life as diocesan priests is charity; for the active and positive love of the holy people of God *is* the apostolate of the bishop and we share in that in a wholly unique and proper way. Now charity is not merely the bond of perfection, it *is* perfection. Our glory as diocesan priests, Father, is that we are not merely "in the way of perfection" but that we *have* perfection. Indeed, as diocesan priests, we do not merely have it, we have it thrust upon us. Herein lies our greatness. Here is our glory.

To summarize, let us impress this lesson by turning to the rite of priestly ordination. We could draw inspiration from the many Scriptural texts bearing on these two truths. But there is always the danger of impersonalizing—"Paul was writing to Timothy, not to me. Peter was addressing the presbyters of his time, not of mine." You cannot impersonalize the words of the rite of ordination: they were addressed personally and directly to *you.* Again and again on that memorable day, Father, you were reminded of these two basic truths about your priesthood: you owe your existence as a diocesan priest to the bishop; your life as a diocesan priest is founded on charity.

First, you owe your existence as a diocesan priest to the bishop. You received your priesthood not just *from* a bishop but *for* a bishop. Listen again to what he told you that day: "Therefore try to be such that, by the grace of God, you may be worthy to be chosen *as a helper* of the Twelve Apostles, that is of the Catholic Bishops . . . And so, dearly beloved son, chosen to be *our helper in the ministry* . . ." Then, during the solemn Preface of Ordination (by Apostolic Constitution declared to be essential to validity) you heard this: "Thou, O God, gave to the Apostles of thy Son helpers to teach the Faith . . . Therefore we ask Thee, O God, to *give us too such help in our ministry.* We need it so much more than they because our infirmity is so much greater than theirs . . . Invest these Thy servants with the dignity of the priesthood; renew in their hearts the spirit of holiness so that they may keep *this office of second rank* they have received from Thee . . . May they be zealous *fellow-laborers of our Order* (*sint providi cooperatores ordinis nostri*)." This successor of the apostles said to the Lord about you: we need them as fellow-laborers of our order. They come into being in relation to our order. This explains *why* they are at all, and *how* they are: "*cooperatores ordinis nostri.*"

And the second great truth: that your life as a diocesan priest is founded on charity. On that day of your ordination you heard the bishop say: "The office of the priest is to offer sacrifice." But in the same breath he added much more: "to baptize, to lead (*prae-esse*), to preach, to bless"—and, implicitly, all the other demands of a ministry of service to the people. A little farther along in that same allocution you heard him say: "Thus the Lord wished to teach by word and deed that the ministers of his Church should be founded upon the twin virtues of charity, namely the love of God and the love of neighbor." Finally, as he placed the chasuble, the garment of your priesthood, over your strong young shoulders you heard him say: "*Accipe vestem sacerdotalem per quam caritas intelligitur*—Receive the garment proper to you as a priest; it is the symbol of charity."

This is your life. Dependent upon and in collaboration with an apostle-bishop, the perfection which is charity is laid across your back. It is thrust upon you. You are, in symbol, completely clothed in it. This is your life and mine, our glory: to belong to the holy people of God in a lifelong ministry of service. There is none greater. It is a life of perfection, for it is a life committed to charity which is perfection.

12. The Diocesan Priesthood: Its Spirituality

WITHOUT A DOUBT, the greatest thing you do as a priest is to offer Holy Mass. It was also the *first* thing you did as a priest. Before you gave your first priestly blessing to your father and mother, before you preached or baptized or absolved, you offered Holy Mass. Literally, you began your priesthood by offering Holy Mass.

But do you remember HOW you offered that first Mass? There is a most significant lesson in how you began your priesthood. You co-offered Mass. You con-celebrated. You offered your first Mass in unison with your bishop! Don't let the real implication of this escape you. This con-celebration was more than a rare ceremony; it was dramatic witness at the very beginning to the central fact about your priesthood: that it is in-collaboration-with the Episcopacy. As a diocesan priest you do not merely offer Holy Mass—you offer Holy Mass *in union with* your bishop. Your first priestly act bore witness to the fact that you became a priest and are a priest only in this context. Your ordination con-celebration set a precedent and underscored a principle. Your vocation as a diocesan priest is "with the bishop."

What began there at your ordination has, in a sense, never

changed. *Every* Mass you have offered since that first one, you have offered in unity with your bishop. You and I must never forget that to celebrate Mass licitly we need more than the power of Orders; we also need "faculties." When we offer Mass in our parishes we do so by virtue of a delegation from our bishop, and in a real sense we do so only in his place and stead. The *"fractio panis"* of the Mass reminds you of this. The rubric of detaching this particle of the Sacred Host, the *"fermentum,"* is kept in our Mass-rite today as a kind of vestigial remain from the days long ago when the *fermentum* was sent out by the bishop to priests celebrating Mass throughout his city-diocese as a sign of their unity with him, as a sign that these priests were offering Mass in his place and in his stead. Your cathedral is your bishop's church and it is, therefore, *the* church of your city-diocese. All others, in a sense, are "mission churches" or "chapels of ease."

That you are the bishop's "other self" is evident not only in the Eucharist but in your every official act: forgiving sins, preaching the word, administering the sacraments. All this you do only by virtue of a delegation from your Ordinary and in his place and stead. And of course, this principle of subordinate collaboration is obvious in all jurisdiction you wield in a parish or administrative appointment. He is the Shepherd. He is the Pastor. You and I are this only as his delegate: we are pastors subalternate.

And let us not be on the defensive because we are called "secular" priests. Rather let us humbly exult in the title. As Doctor Parente points out in his introduction to Canon Masure's book on the diocesan priesthood, the Church calls us "secular priests" rather than "diocesan priests" in the Code of Canon Law and in her official documents. "Secular," of course, refers to "saeculum," the world. Now isn't that exactly where Christ wanted his priests? "Go you into the whole *world* and preach the gospel to every creature (Mark 16:16) . . . I do not pray (Father) that thou take them out of the world but that thou keep them from evil" (John

17:15). This is our proudest boast, Father, that we are "secular" priests. We are sent to men living in the world, exposed to the attacks of Satan. We are incarnate among the children of men. Our calling is to be at the side of God's holy people who are in the arena for the supreme test, through Baptism entered into the lists against the Prince of this world.

And this was Christ's way: He became IN-CARNATE. No remote-control system for the salvation of men has yet been devised. We secular priests are in the arena of this world, at the side of our brothers on the front line of battle, day and night at the beck and call of God's holy and bothersome people, at the expense of rest and comfort and personal preference and good order and study and, yes, even of prayer. This is our life, Father, as secular priests—as the proper helpers and auxiliaries of bishops, of those who were sent as He was sent: "not to be ministered unto but to minister" (Matt. 20:28). It is a chaotic life; at times perhaps even a little idiotic. But that is the way with charity: "fools for the sake of Christ" (I Cor. 4:10). And you know, Father, there is no higher life. Charity is perfection, and since our life as secular priests is founded on charity, our state is a state of perfection: a perfection of service under the bishop.

As diocesan priests we are the *proper* helpers of an apostle-bishop. It is we who are, properly and authentically, his "other selves." Therefore we are not merely *committed* to charity, we are *married* to it. Through and in our bishop, we secular priests are married to the people of God, the Church. This is why the bishop wears a ring. The episcopal ring is a wedding ring. The bishop of a diocese belongs to the people of his Church by virtue of an indissoluble bond analagous to the *vinculum matrimoniale*. To this day Papal Bulls dealing with the transfer of a bishop from one See to another speak of its taking effect *"vinculo soluto"*—that is, after the loosing of the bond which bound him to the people of his Diocese or Church. This conjugal analogy is explicitly underscored in the handing over of the ring in the rite of episcopal consecration: "Receive this ring, symbol of fidelity, in order that you may unfalteringly guard the spouse of God, namely His holy Church." Of course, the inspiration for this typology is the rich biblical allusion to the Church as "the bride of Christ," soaring to its most eloquent pitch in the passages from Ephesians incorporated into the Rite of Matrimony and the Nuptial Mass. As a diocesan priest, by virtue of your unique relationship to your bishop, you are a partner in this marital contract even more directly and personally than religious priests. Through and in your bishop you are married to charity; you are married to the people of God whom you serve. Ministering to these people, providing for their spiritual sustenance, protecting them, working your heart out for them: this is your *proper calling* as a secular priest.

To say that our calling as secular priests is inferior is to say that the Episcopacy is inferior. To say that our vocation to the diocesan priesthood is inferior is to say that charity is inferior.

Father, you and I must be saints. We must be saints *because* we are secular priests. *How* we are to be I cannot tell you. But this much we must know: there is nothing second-rate about our calling; there is nothing second-best about our way. The first step toward becoming the saints we must be is to recognize what we are. Cardinal Suhard wrote: "The first thing a priest must do to lead a priestly life is to realize that he is a priest, to become more and more aware of the priesthood with which he has been invested." We are allowed the paraphrase: "The first thing the secular priest must do to lead a priestly life is to realize that he is a secular priest, to become more and more aware of the secular priesthood with which he has been invested." Too long, Father, have we taken the attitude that we are the country cousins, the poor second-raters who couldn't quite make the grade to complete dedication by the religious vows! A second-rate outlook produces second-raters at best. Let us not be narrow or divisive or odiously comparative. Let there be no prejudice among us against the lofty ideals of the religious priesthood. But neither let us secular priests take the attitude that we must somehow apologize for our state.

I cannot tell you how to become a saint. I can tell you only that *your calling as a secular priest demands it!* We must go back to the theology of the Christian priesthood and thus be deeply aware that there is nothing inferior about our participation in it, for the simple reason that there is nothing superior to charity. How we are to achieve this sanctity I know not; but I do know that we shall never achieve it if we never aspire to it. And to aspire to it means simply to be aware of who and what and why we are, of what and why the secular priesthood is. Call it what you will: morale, *esprit de corps*. What is essential is that we must be deeply and humbly and gratefully aware of what we are. We have to realize that "the greatest of these is charity" (I Cor. 13:13). Enough of puerile squaring-off of secular versus religious. More power to our religious brother-priests for the fine sense of the utter sublimity of the calling they possess. Pray God they never lose it! But let's have done with the assumption, especially the assumption by us, that *our* calling is inferior. We secular priests may have perfectly warranted misgivings about the way we as individuals measure up to this calling of ours, but under no circumstances let us ever belittle the calling itself. We ourselves are the losers if we do.

Whatever our spirituality as secular priests is to be, it must begin from here. It must be firmly anchored in out-going charity. All the warnings about the "heresy of activism" must be fully heeded. None of the wisdom about the importance of the "interior life" can be ignored. But this horrible dichotomy between the "interior life" and positive charity in our priestly ministry must go. Most of us regard it as more than a dichotomy—we see it as open antagonism. Most of us were trained to regard the works of our active priestly ministry as tainted and somehow destructive of real sanctity. The tension this creates in our lives can be almost unbearable. Our key to bona fide sanctity lies in erasing this dichotomy and in eliminating this tension. We can do neither so long as that charity toward our brethren to which we have been called and for which we exist as secular priests is given anything less than first place in our lives. As secular priests, sent not to be ministered unto but to minister, we have got to see that for us to become saints is not so much a case of sanctifying the things we do, as simply allowing them to sanctify us. Our calling is charity, and charity is perfection. We do not have to make what we do holy. Our problem is to let it make us holy.

Our problem as secular priests is to be aware that to sit in a lovely, quiet chapel chanting the Divine Office is not necessarily holier or more sanctifying than to sit captive for two hours in the rectory office, listening to the endless inanities of some unconscionable bore who could not continue to love God except for this good-natured slob here, willing not only to hear her out, but willing to have a perfectly promising afternoon completely queered.

Our problem is to see that scrupulous adherence to the holy vow of poverty is not necessarily holier or more sanctifying than reaching into your pocket to give a buck to the bum at the rectory door, through whose cock-and-bull story you can see 100 percent.

Our problem as secular priests is to recognize that teaching theology to mature students in some great university is not necessarily holier or more sanctifying than teaching the simple good news of Christ's redemption to addle-brained little monsters in the third grade of parochial school.

Our problem as secular priests is to find the faith to understand that writing a meditation manual for nuns is not necessarily holier or more sanctifying than writing the annual financial report for the Chancery Office.

Our problem as priests in the world is to have the faith to see that marching in stately liturgical procession into some fine church is not necessarily holier or more sanctifying than marching shoulder-to-shoulder with our oppressed brothers in a littered city street to secure their God-given human dignity.

Our problem as secular priests is to appreciate that keeping the holy rule in an orderly religious house is not necessarily holier or more sanctifying than simply keeping your sanity in the maddening disorder of a busy parish rectory, under unrelenting assault day and night through telephone and doorbell by God's holy people.

Our problem is to realize that getting up in the middle of the night to go chant Matins is not necessarily holier or more sanctifying than getting up in the middle of the night to go anoint a sick member of Christ's Body.

Our problem is to recognize that visiting Christ in the Blessed Sacrament at our convenience is not necessarily holier or more sanctifying than visiting Christ in a home to which we have at immense inconvenience been summarily called to arbitrate a domestic quarrel.

All this and much more is our problem as secular priests: priests in the world, priests among men. Our problem is to grasp the truth of St. Paul's ascetical axiom: "Bear you one another's burdens, and thus *fulfill* the law of Christ" (Gal. 6:2)—an axiom which the Church thrusts upon our attention again and again throughout the week in the canonical hour of Sext. And how appropriate for us parish priests the *lectio brevis* for Prime: "May the Lord direct our hearts and our bodies into the charity of God and unto the patience of Christ." Yes, may the patience of Christ show us the way—especially on Sunday when we get that umpteenth phone call from one of God's holy people wanting to know "what time is your next Mass." How ingenious of the Church to have selected this as a *lectio brevis* for *Sunday!* Father, as secular priests we are married to the people of God, *all* of them: the devout and the apathetic, the appreciative and the ungrateful, the "nice people" and the "screwballs." As secular priests our life is to serve them and to minister unto them "without distinction of persons" (I Peter 1:17). All of us have long since discovered that nothing is more disordering, disappointing, disenchanting, distracting than this. What we must also discover is that nothing is holier, more ennobling, more sanctifying than this! This *is* charity: charity not in some glamorous daydream or in some lovely ivory tower, but flesh and blood devotion to flesh and blood mankind. It is perfection, Father. There is nothing greater. "Bear you one another's burdens and thus fulfill the law of Christ" (Gal. 6:2). "If you love one another then you have God dwelling in you and the love of God will have reached its full growth in your life" (I John 4:12). This is our life as secular priests, as priests in the world, priests among men. We must have the faith to accept this calling and thus to give ourselves up to it. This we must do not only for our own sanctification, but for the very salvation of "the people whom God means to have for His own" (I Peter 2:9).

However it is to develop, this charity, *agape,* is the matrix of an authentic spirituality for us diocesan priests. The details will have to be filled in by "elders" or presbyters from our own ranks, men wiser and holier and more practical and more experienced than we. But we can at least make a reliable beginning by keeping clearly before our minds the two essential points of departure:

First, in the sure light of authentic theology which links us so directly with the Episcopacy, to start from a deep reverence for the unexcelled sublimity of our secular priesthood. We must set out bodly from the firm conviction that there is no calling higher or greater than our secular priesthood—whatever our personal deficiencies in measuring up may be at any given point.

Secondly, we must start from an unabashed acceptance of charity. We must once-and-for-all commit ourselves to committing ourselves to God's people, with all the crazy demands this demands of us. To be true to our calling as secular priests we must be completely willing to make absolutely everything else subordinate to charity, both in theory and in fact. We have got to realize that there is no other reason for our existence—and then respond to the grace to live and act accordingly.

These are our points of departure. The details remain to be supplied, but these are the touchstones of an asceticism for secular priests. One of the major details to be filled in will be our relationship as diocesan priests to Mary, the holy mother of the Lord. I suppose we are tempted at times to feel just slightly left out. We "plain-vanilla" secular priests can lay claim to no *special* marks of her favor as so many of our religious brethren do. Everybody knows it was not to us *secular* priests Our Lady entrusted the brown scapular—or the green one or the red one or the white one or the black one. You name it, we don't have it! Everybody knows it was not to a secular priest the Lady of the Rosary taught the beads. Everybody knows it was not upon us secular priests the Madonna of the Miraculous Medal smiled her smile. Everybody knows it was not to the likes of us the Sorrowful Mother entrusted her riches, or to us she bared her Immaculate Heart. No, not to us any visions or apparitions or revelations or miraculous signs of favor or trust.

Yet, isn't this as it should be? If we secular priests are true to our proper calling and minding our knitting, we are too immersed in the poor people we serve to see the Blessed Mother! We are in plain fact too busy and too distracted to indulge the luxury of visions. When it is an insistently ringing telephone you have to hear all day long, it's kind of hard for private revelations to come through! We hear private revelations, indeed loads of them—but most of them are the kind that would make the Blessed Mother's hair stand on end!

Perhaps it is just as well we secular priests have no *private* revelations on which to peg our devotion to the Blessed Mother. To discover *ours* we are forced to go back to *public* revelation, Sacred Scripture, and to straight theology. And I submit that, after all, these sources are rather hard to improve upon.

What do they tell us, theology and the Bible? They tell us, in the first place, that Jesus Christ is the only Priest. He shared his unique priesthood directly with the Apostles and their successors and with no one else. They in turn shared it with the presbyterate, with the kind of priests you and I are. But they share it with us *diocesan* priests by a participation which is quite personal and direct. *All* priests, religious and secular, share in the priesthood given the apostles-bishops. But we share in it in a unique and special way.

Now it was by the Incarnation that Christ became the one, the only priest. Granted "God's loving design," Jesus Christ could not have become this priest without our Lady. It is precisely as "true God *and* true man" that he is Priest. Mary is the mother of this God-man. Mary is the only mother of the only Priest. Her relationship to him as Priest is not a moral relationship as on Calvary: her relationship to him as Priest is physical, essential, indispensable. Because we are diocesan priests, the proper "other selves" of an apostle-bishop, you and I stand in a unique and proper relationship to her.

Conscious of this special birthright of ours, and realizing that we have no private revelations of our own from her, we go to Holy Writ itself to discover what she wished to say to us. We find there that her recorded words dwindle down to a precious few. As St. Bernardinus points out in the second nocturn for the feast of her Immaculate Heart, she spoke only seven times for posterity. The Holy Spirit saw fit to give us only seven words of Mary in all of public revelation. She talked twice with the Archangel, twice with Elizabeth, twice with her Son (in the

temple and at Cana) and once with the waiters at Cana. Her last
recorded words in public revelation were addressed to ordinary
waiters. They are, in a sense, her last will and testament. They
are most interesting, most significant. The Only Priest whom she
mothered is about to begin the public exercise of his ministry. Immediately before it begins, this last time she speaks—and after this
all is silence. What she says is more than a statement, it is a di-
rective, a command—as far as we know, the only one she ever
uttered. It is a summation of true devotion to Mary. Do you remember those words, Father? Five little words, with the wisdom
of heaven behind them: "Do whatever he tells you" (John 2:5).
This is what our Blessed Mother wants to say to us. This is her
own personal, authentic prescription for true Marian piety: "Do
whatever my Son tells you."

Because of our unique relationship to him as diocesan priests,
we above all must be willing to do whatever he tells us. We recall
that he once said of his Church: "he who hears you hears me."
To discover what he tells us we look to what the Church tells
us. Through the Church, in Canon 125, he tells us to pray Mary's
rosary daily. We must take this seriously. We dare not ignore it
or flub it.

Priests have come to me to tell me that they cannot pray the
rosary. Its hypnotic monotony and maddening repetition defeat true
attention, and they look askance at its prayer-wheel ideology. They
argue that because of this proven impossibility of *praying* it they
see no point in their *saying* it. I must confess that I did not always have an answer. But I have one now. I got it the day Pope
John XXIII died. That night NBC television showed a docu-
mentary on the life of this great and good man. Everyone who
saw it was deeply moved by it. But one thing in particular moved
me. I shall never forget it. There on the screen was this beloved
shepherd, surrounded by his immediate household, kneeling in his
chapel—saying the beads. The commentator said he did this every

day of his life. Father, are we busier than he? Are we spiritually more sophisticated than he? More advanced in sanctity? If the rosary was good enough for Pope John, it should be good enough for us!

13. Approaches to Holy Mass

FOR A LONG TIME books and conferences for priests treated the Mass as sort of our own private preserve. We put so much emphasis on what it should mean to us that we forgot to make it meaningful for the people. Needless to say there were some rather strange results from this "my Mass" approach, because the Mass has *no* meaning apart from the holy people of God. Lately, however, the pendulum has swung the other way. We read and hear so much about "the people's Mass" that some of us may be excused for wondering whether the priest has any stake in it at all. Needless to say there can also be some rather strange results from this "people's Mass" approach, because the Mass not only has no meaning, it has no existence apart from the priest. I am all in favor of stressing the ecclesial dimension of the Mass, but we must maintain a true perspective and neither diminish nor dilute our own unique and essential role in this central act of Christian worship.

Let us therefore consider some aspects of the priest's approach to his one supreme priestly act: Holy Mass.

First of all, how do we come to it? How are we cast? What is our role in it? There is no more authentic guide than the Mass itself. And what does the Mass tell you? When you talk about yourself in

Holy Mass, *how* do you? What do you call yourself? Priest? *Sacerdos?* Not at all—not even once! *Presbyter?* Or *praeses?* No, not that either. You mention yourself often during the course of the Mass: occasionally in the first person singular, many times (as part of the assembly) in the first person plural. But as far as I know you mention *yourself and the assembly separately* only four times: in the offering of the bread, the *Hanc Igitur,* the *Unde et memores* and the *Placeat.* These are the only instances when you make an explicit distinction between yourself and the people. And in these four instances what do you call yourself? At the Offertory it is "*famulus*" and in the other three references it is "*servus.*"

How profoundly significant this is! Your priestly power and your authority over the Christian community reach their highest expression in the Mass, yet in relation to that community you speak of yourself only as slave or servant! Dare I observe here that when bishops and archbishops celebrate Holy Mass they say the same thing and speak of themselves the same way—and so even do pastors! And dare I observe further that this concept of our priestly role expressed here brings *all* of us, priests and bishops, face to face with a major problem in the Church today? We are so imbued with the idea of authority that it is all but impossible for us to grasp and to take seriously the meaning of "ministry."

How significant that Vatican Council II has now officially dropped the term "monarchical hierarchy." We fervently hope that they drop more than the term. How significant that for the first one-thousand years the work of bishops and priests was known simply as the "*diakonia,*" the ministry. Father Jungmann reminds us that in the New Testament the term "*hieros*" or priest is applied only to Christ and to the people of God, never to bishops and presbyters. In *Mediator Dei* Pius XII makes it clear that only the words of Consecration belong exclusively to the priest. All the rest, even the strictly sacerdotal prayers as well as the Eucharistic Prayer itself, is said in the name of the Christian people. Though these are actually said only by the priest they are, in the words of the Constitution, said "in the name of the entire holy people and of all present" (Par. 33). It is just possible that there is no more urgent business in the Church today than for you and me to re-examine our role as minister or servant to the Christian community.

No Pope in modern history brought greater prestige to the authority of the papacy than John XXIII, yet none gave more eloquent witness to the world of what it means to be *"pater et pastor et minister."* The Christ of the gospels who could say "All authority in heaven and on earth has been given to me" (Matt. 28:18), is the same Christ who said "I stand in the midst of you as one who serves" (Luke 22:27) ". . . I have come not to be ministered unto but to minister" (Mark 10:45). It is just possible that the one fact about our vocation we priests and bishops need most to rediscover today is the ancient but simple truth that we have been called by God out of the Christian community not to *boss* it but to *serve* it. And there is a subtle hazard in including bishops here, because it is so attractive for us priests to see the speck of sawdust in the bishop's eye and not to notice the two-by-four in our own eye. In our own more modest sphere and in our own modest way, some of us succeed in making some of them look like mere toddlers in tyranny. A pastor with his people, or with his assistants, who talks about *"running my* parish" and who does exactly that! Or an assistant priest, maybe only with the altar boys—but, boy, does he rule *them* with an iron fist! A famous and respected American priest (who is in fact too famous and too respected for me to identify here) says he is convinced that clerical bossism has caused greater scandal and wrought more harm in the Church than clerical fornication.

Ite ad Missam! Go to the Mass, where your presidency over the holy people of God is so clearly defined, where your unique power in the Christian community is so immediately obvious. Learn your lesson there. Take seriously what you say there: *ego famulus, nos servi.* Each of us should ponder from time to time how phony these fine words sound coming from us at Mass. We must let the Mass teach us what He tried to teach us: "Whoever would be first among you must become the servant of all . . . even as the Son of Man" (Mark 10:43).

Secondly, let us reflect on the truth that for us priests the approach to Holy Mass must be an approach through faith and hope and charity.

We must approach it with faith. I am sure that you have deep faith in what *you* do there. But I wonder, do you also have deep faith in what *the assembly* does there? You approach with magnificent faith the real presence of Christ which *you* bring about there. But do you approach with equal faith the real presence of Christ which *the assembly* brings about there? You believe in the mystery of Christ's real presence on the corporal; but do you believe in the mystery of Christ's real presence in the pews? I do not mean to sound blasphemous, but I am convinced that in a certain way we have made too much of the Lord's real presence in the Blessed Sacrament. We have restricted and narrowed down his really real presence exclusively to that particular one. That real presence, I know, is an entirely unique one. But it does not exhaust the mode or manner of the Lord's real presence among us. We have no right so to confine Him.

And we are suffering the consequences of this narrow concept of real presence: our people simply do not see what the Christian assembly is and, therefore, they do not understand what the Church is or what the Eucharist is. Our Catholic people have no effective faith in the mystery of that real-presence-of-Christ which they bring about by their very assembly. And *they* haven't it because *we* haven't it—they get it only from us. One practical consequence of this lack of faith is their refusal even to form an assembly. Have you ever noticed how instinctively they scatter themselves throughout the church for week-day Mass? It is sheer lack of space and nothing else which forces them to "gather together" for the celebra-

tion of the Eucharist on Sunday. Like a famous actress of a genera-
tion ago, they "want to be alone." There is a time and a place to be
alone with God, but the celebration of the Christian Eucharist is
neither that time nor that place. Something is radically wrong
when they refuse to gather into one for the offering of Him who
came precisely "that he might gather into one the children of God
who were scattered" (John 11:52).

Another practical consequence of this lack of faith in "real presence" is the immense difficulty we experience in getting them to
participate in Mass as a community. They will not because they
have no sense of community. And they never will have it unless and
until you and I have it. We have got to take and meditate deeply on
that one little sentence in paragraph 7 of the Constitution: "Christ
is present when the Church prays and sings, for he promised:
'Where two or three are gathered together in my name, there am I
in the midst of them.' " He *is* present because when this assembly
forms it is *his body,* the Church. It is not a decapitated body: Christ
is its head and he *is* present. But you are its acting head—you stand
as the *visible* head of this really-present body of Christ. The visible
sign of *this* real presence of the Lord is not the Host—it is *you!*
Thus the Constitution says "Christ is present in the sacrifice of the
Mass *in the person of His minister*" (Par. 7). Now if you do not
have faith in this real presence, it becomes rather difficult for you to
signify or cause faith in this real presence.

At first blush this sounds like some kind of disparagement of the
Eucharist. But this too is the Eucharist! This is not just *any*
assembly—this is the Eucharistic assembly. There is a profound con-
nection between the Blessed Sacrament and the Eucharistic assembly.
The Greek word *"synaxis"* means assembly, and for hundreds of
years *"synaxis"* was the word used for the Blessed Sacrament in the
Eastern Church. Father de Lubac points out that for a thousand
years *"Corpus Christi Mysticum"* (the Mystical Body of Christ)
meant the Blessed Sacrament, and that only later did it come to

mean the Church or assembly. Of course, our own word "Communion" is significant: liturgically it means the Blessed Sacrament, but semantically it means congregation or assembly. We must not let the "me and Jesus" approach to Holy Communion blind us to the truth that our people *receive* the Body of Christ so that they can *be* the body of Christ. Come to think of it, I wonder why we talk about "receiving Holy Communion" anyway? Semantically this phrase doesn't make sense. To speak of "achieving" Holy Communion rather than "receiving" Holy Communion is not only better syntax, it is decidedly better theology. Neither we nor our Catholic people appreciate the intimate relationship between the Eucharistic assembly and the Eucharistic sacrament. It was not always thus. That key third-century document, the *Didascalia Apostolorum,* counsels bishops to urge the people not to absent themselves from the assembly lest thereby the body of Christ be diminished and lack one of its members (quoted in Jungmann's *The Early Liturgy*). We priests must re-discover this faith in our Lord's real presence, bring it to the parish Mass and communicate it to His holy people.

Your approach to Holy Mass is also an approach through hope. We know well enough that the Mass is the *"mysterium fidei"* and we readily recognize the place of faith in the Mass. But we must also recognize the place of hope in the Mass: it is also the *"mysterium spei."* Every Mass is alight with the glory of the "endtime." If hope be not the first, then certainly it is the final purpose of every Mass. Every Mass is indeed a solemn recalling to mind of the saving acts of the past; every Mass is also a present-time here-and-now application of these saving acts. But just as surely, every Mass awakens our hope in that future-time when salvation shall have been accomplished. In fact it is precisely this future-time, this object of hope, which is the whole point and goal and purpose of our re-calling the past salvific acts and of our making them present. If hope be not the first, then surely it is the final purpose of every Mass.

For the Christian, hope is not crassly individualistic. It is essentially communal. The Christian hopes because the Church hopes. The individual Christian is taking part in a pilgrimage en route home to the Father.

Now it is at Mass that this communal Christian hope takes on flesh and becomes vivid and real and existentialized. "The Church which hopes" is too big an idea for our people to grasp. "The Church which hopes" is but poorly envisaged as some gigantic world-wide body to which we feel only vaguely that we "belong." It is the Mass which cuts this splendid vision down to our size and scope. At Mass "the Church which hopes" is none other than *this* church, consisting of these faithful gathered together in this building and assembled around this priest. At Mass "the hope of the Church" takes on flesh and becomes *our* hope, in a real and existential way. At Mass it is *this* assembly—*nos servi tui et plebs tua sancta*—which is recalling to mind God's saving acts of the past and which is actually experiencing His love in here-and-now redemption. It is *this* assembly which reacts in hope to this recollection-of-the-past and to this application-in-the-present. And it is a hope communally experienced. Hope literally surges through this existential assembly and rises from it like a wave. This *is* the Church hoping!

And so, at Mass, we express our hope and we pray for its fulfillment. Again and again this assembly expresses its prayerful yearning for salvation. Two instances stand out as particularly vivid and touching. In the Memento for the Living we say in the name of the people: "Remember, Lord . . . all who are assembled here around your altar. You know their commitment and surrender (*fides et devotio*) . . . They offer to You this sacrifice of praise . . . for the salvation in which they hope (*pro spe salutis*)." This communal yearning for our true home reaches childlike poignancy in the *Nobis Quoque Peccatoribus,* a prayer born of homesickness, a plea issuing from the whole assembly: "We your sinful servants have hope, O Lord, in your boundless mercy. Please give us part and fellowship with your holy apostles and martyrs . . . and all your saints. We beg You, let us share their company . . ."

But so irrepressible is this communal hope at Mass that the assembly not only expresses it in prayerful yearning but actually resorts to liturgical role-playing to make it real and palpable and, as it were, already achieved. This occurs twice: at the *Sanctus* and at the Communion.

The whole meaning of the *Sanctus* derives from the *Parousia*—the *Parousia* acted out. At the *Sanctus* the entire assembly actually anticipates its hope as already accomplished: "The hosts of heaven join with the holy Seraphim in a hymn of celebration. We ask that our voices may join in too, as all together we sing out joyfully: Holy, Holy, Holy, Lord God of Sabaoth."

The same anticipatory play-acting occurs at Communion—though it is safe to say that of all the truths about Communion we do not see, this is the one we see least. Now it should be obvious enough that hope is intimately connected with Holy Communion because we say so every time we take it: "May the Body of our Lord Jesus Christ keep my soul *unto life everlasting*." And we know well enough that Communion is not only the "*sacrum convivium in quo Christus sumitur*" but also "*in quo futurae gloriae nobis pignus datur*" (Hymn of St. Thomas Aquinas). But the mystery of the banquet meal runs deeper than this in the Christian experience. In both scripture and tradition it not only points to glory, but is the type or figure par excellence *of glory itself*. Our most common and most authentic figure of heaven itself is the wedding banquet in the new Jerusalem. Scripture and tradition are saturated with this particular typology. Among our most important monuments from Christian antiquity are certain frescoes in the catacombs depicting a meal or banquet. For a long time it was assumed that these were representations of Communion, the Eucharistic meal, in the early Church. But more careful study reveals that they are Christian art's primitive attempts to portray not the Eucharistic meal on earth but the wedding banquet in the heavenly Jerusalem. This typology of "the heavenly wedding feast" is explicit in our rite of Baptism. At the Communion of the Mass the people partake of the Sacred Banquet together. They not only receive a pledge of future glory, they act out what it pledges them: not hope as such, but the actual consummation of hope. At the *Sanctus* of the Mass the assembly's hope bursts through in acting out the typology of the heavenly choirs. At the Communion of the Mass their hope issues in an acting out of the typology of the heavenly wedding feast.

The Constitution, by the way, underscores the place of hope in the Mass by devoting an entire paragraph to it: "In the earthly liturgy we take part in a *foretaste* of that heavenly liturgy celebrated in the holy city of Jerusalem, toward which we journey as pilgrims . . . We sing a hymn to the Lord's glory with all the warriors of the heavenly army; venerating the memory of the saints we hope for some part and fellowship with them" (Par. 8). Father, you lead this pilgrimage as you stand at the head of the assembly. Therefore this is a hope *you* must have before it can become a hope *they* will have.

Finally, your approach to Holy Mass is an approach in charity. You must come to the altar as a man in love.

At least once during their lives most of our Catholic people come to at least one Mass very much in love. It is their Nuptial Mass. The love they bring to this Mass is, in fact, so strong that it results in their making a covenant.

Well, every Mass is a Nuptial Mass. Every Mass, at its point of deepest meaning, is the making of a covenant—the New Covenant. "This *is* the New Covenant in my blood" (I Cor. 11:25). Every Mass is the making of a love-covenant between the Bridegroom and his Spouse, the Church. Every Mass is the making of a love-covenant between our Lord Jesus Christ and *this* assembly or church present around the altar.

Scripture and tradition give us two predominant figures to express the Christian mystery: the figure of the Body of Christ (Head and members), and the figure of the nuptial covenant. During the past forty or fifty years we have rediscovered and plumbed the depths of the first, the Body-figure. The "Mystical Body of Christ theme" has dominated our theological thought. To say that we have been enormously enriched by its insights is a gross understatement. However, signs are increasing that we may be approaching a new era: to plumb the depths and tap the riches of the second figure: the nuptial figure. The Fathers of Vatican Council II, significantly, chose *this* one in writing their introduction to the Constitution's important Chapter Two, on "The Most Sacred Mystery of the Eucharist." Christ entrusts "to *his beloved spouse,* the Church, a memorial of his death and resurrection: a sacrament of love, a sign of unity, a bond of charity . . ." (Par. 47).

The New Covenant is nothing more or less than marriage between the *Son* of God and the *people* of God. Essentially the Church is a marriage. This marriage took place at the Last Supper. We teach that the Church came into being atop Calvary out of the riven side of the sacrificed Lord. But what happened there in the historical order had "already" happened in the sacramental order at the Last Supper. Jesus did not say at the Supper: "This cup *will be* the New Covenant in my blood." He said: "This cup *is* the New Covenant." This *is* the marriage.

The Mass which you now offer together with your people is not merely a *memorial* of that marriage, it *is* that marriage. At Sunday Mass in your parish the Lord says through you: "This cup *is* the New Covenant in my blood." What is more, when he says that now (at Sunday Mass), *both* parties to the covenant are present. Both parties to this marriage are there. It is not a marriage by proxy. Mark you, what is effected here is not a unilateral covenant, imposed only from above. It is bilateral. The Mass you and God's people offer *is* a marriage—but it is not a "shot-gun marriage." The yes-saying is completely mutual! The marital consent is real, it is free, it is born of mutual love. The New Covenant is nothing if it is not a love pact. This divine Bridegroom not only gives himself to his Bride. The Bride too says "I will," the Bride too gives herself in loving return. "The Bride" is this assembly, this people gathered round you here whom the Lord "means to have for his very own." They bring "*fides et devotio*" to this bilateral covenant. Their "*fides*" is the kind of faith which implies total commitment. Their "*devotio*" is complete personal and communal surrender. These holy people of God bring their response to God in Sunday Mass. They bring their "yes." They come to Mass very much in love.

Because you represent them and speak for them in this love-covenant, you above all must come to it very much in love. For you and me the Mass we offer must become a real, conscious, free yes-saying to the Christ who gives himself for us and to us. This is no empty dream. This is not only what every parish Mass *should* be—this is what every parish Mass *can* and *must* be. When the Mass does indeed become this, then you and I shall stand at the head of God's holy people and lead them in that great corporate "Amen" to His Son's own self-giving which every Mass is intended to be. Then indeed will the Mass be what the Constitution says it is: "a sacrament of love, a sign of unity, a bond of charity." Then indeed we shall have put meaning and guts into those staggering words: "This is the New Covenant in my blood."

14. Praying the Breviary

THE CHURCH has got to pray. From this there is no dispensation. The Church is Christ incarnate in today's world. The Church is "Jesus Christ spread abroad and passed on—the permanent incarnation of the Son of God" (Bossuet). "God made him the head to which the whole Church is joined, so that the Church is his body, the completion of him" (Eph. 1:23). The Church, as this "completion of Christ," carries on and completes the work of Christ in the world today. And what was "the work of Christ?" By his death, resurrection and ascension to atone for our sins, make us partakers of the divine nature and return us to the Father? Yes. But this was not his only work. As a matter of fact, this was not even his primary work. We have his own word for it that the redemption of man was not the first purpose of his coming. At the Last Supper he turned to his Father and said: "I have glorified you on earth; I have finished the work you gave me to do" (John 17:4). This above all was his mission: to glorify God on earth. To render worship, praise and adoration to the Father was "the work" his Father had given him to do.

Because the Church is Christ-completing-his-work in the world today, the Church must render worship, praise and adoration to the Father. We are woefully short of the mark if we regard her work of salvation as the exclusive or even the paramount mission of the Church. Because the Church is Christ, the primary work of the Church is the same as the primary work of Christ: to glorify God on earth. Nor is it enough to say that God is glorified in every man who is saved. Of course he is. But there is more to it than this. The work of rendering praise and adoration to the Godhead is also and necessarily a distinct and essential duty of the Church. Really to understand the Mass is to see this aspect of worship as a primary and essential feature. The Mass is not just *"sacrificium"* but specifically *"sacrificium laudis."* This is true of all the sacraments, of the entire liturgy. *"Sacramenta propter homines"* we say—but we must never say it in prejudice to the more essential truth: *"Sacramenta propter Deum."* In a true and real sense the primary purpose of *every* sacrament, even of the sacrament of Penance, is the worship of God, and only subordinately the salvation of man. Inherent in every liturgical act of the Church is the absolute primacy of divine worship. This is why the Constitution on the Sacred Liturgy describes the liturgy as "this great work wherein God is perfectly glorified and men are sanctified" (Par. 7).

But not even this is enough. The Church, permanent incarnation of the praying and adoring Christ, has instituted a special medium through which to carry on the primary work assigned her: the work of praise. It is her "Godly Duty"—the Divine Office. The Office is the extra-precautionary means adopted by the Church lest her primary work suffer either from lack of emphasis or lack of doing. There is an eminence and dignity to the Divine Office which we must not ignore. Its reason for being is identical with THE work of the Church. If object or purpose determines nature, then we must admit that in a sense the Divine Office cedes priority or importance to nothing the Church does. Without qualification, the Constitution on the Sacred Liturgy calls it simply "the greatest honor of Christ's spouse" (Par. 85).

Paragraph 83 of the Constitution introduces the chapter on the

Divine Office and sets forth what we might call "the theology of
the Divine Office." I quote it in full: "Christ Jesus, high priest of the
new and eternal covenant, taking human nature, introduced into
this earthly exile that hymn which is sung throughout all ages in
the halls of heaven. He joins the entire community of mankind to
Himself, associating it with His own singing of this canticle of
divine praise. For he continues his priestly work through the agency
of his Church, which is ceaselessly engaged in praising the Lord
and interceding for the salvation of the whole world. She does this
not only by celebrating the eucharist but also in other ways, especially by praying the divine office." Notice the theology of this text.
Christ's priestly work is pre-eminently his "singing of this canticle
of divine praise." He continues his priestly work through the con-
tinuation of himself: the Church. And the Church continues Christ's
priestly work in two ways: "by praising the Lord and interceding
for the salvation of the whole world." Christ's priestly work is first
of all to praise the Lord God—only secondly is it "the salvation of
the whole world." *This* work, first of praise and secondly of salvation, the Church does through the Eucharist, "but also in other ways,
especially by praying the divine office."

There is a burgeoning interest in the Breviary throughout the
Church today. Laymen in ever increasing numbers are discovering
and using the Divine Office. Vernacular translations and "short
forms" abound. Wonderful! *Intende et prospere procede!*

Yet, something is lacking in this. When *they* take up the Breviary
it is not the same as when *we* do. (Try as I may to have no part in
the clerical habit of referring to the laity as "they," here there really
is no choice.) On their own, the Catholic laity participate only un-
officially and non-liturgically in this primary work of the Church.
And this brings us to a major truth about this work of praise we
call the Divine Office. It is the PRAYER OF THE CHURCH.
There is about it something markedly official and authentic. The
Church does not leave this work of praise to chance, or even to the

fervor of her members. She entrusts it to a carefully selected few and she commissions these to do it under pain of serious sin: monks, certain religious and all those in major orders. In this solicitude you detect more than an acknowledgement of its importance—you see the truth that this is the prayer of the Church herself. All members of the Church are to pray, but it is those of us delegated and set apart by the Church for this work who constitute the *"vox sponsae,"* the "praying Church." This is a truth of the first magnitude and its corollaries are vast.

First among them is the profound truth that this is the PRAYER OF CHRIST. When you and I take up that book, Father, it is not really we who pray, it is Christ who prays. This is the prayer of the Church: the Church who is the permanent incarnation of the Son of God. We have not merely been delegated *by* the Church to do this work of praise, we have been delegated to *be* the Church doing this work of praise and consequently to be Christ-in-today's-world doing this work of praise. The Constitution on the Sacred Liturgy puts it this way: "When this wonderful song of praise is rightly performed by priests and others deputed for this purpose . . . or by the faithful praying (it) together with the priest in the approved form, then it is truly the voice of the bride addressed to her bridegroom; it is the very prayer which Christ himself . . . addresses to the Father" (Par. 84). Aside from the pertinent point that this is the prayer of Christ himself, notice that it is we who are "deputed for this purpose" who constitute this Christ-praising-the-Father. Notice too that the faithful participate liturgically in this work only when they pray the Office "together with the priest in the approved form"—e.g. parish Vespers—and not when they pray the breviary on their own.

Another important corollary is that the Divine Office is PUBLIC PRAYER. You are not alone when you pray the Breviary alone. One with you is the Church—the thousands like you delegated to this work. One with you is Christ who is the pray-er here. Regardless of how privately you and I pray the Breviary, this is a public work we perform. Because it is, not only does none of us pray it *by* himself, he does not pray it *for* himself. When you pray this prayer you are Christ, the one Mediator, praying for and in the name of and in the stead of the tired mothers and the busy fathers and the lazy or involved children and the careless, apathetic, non-praying people of God. And when you are too busy or too apathetic to pray it, some busy, tired, distracted, sleeply priest is praying it for you and in your name and in your stead!

All of us are grateful that the Office has been mercifully shortened. Most of us heartily welcome the opportunity to pray Christ's prayer in our own language. All of us look forward to the full-fledged reform of the Breviary ordered by the Constitution. But let us be honest. Let us be consistent. If we welcome the shortened breviary or the vernacular breviary, let us be just as enthusiastic in accepting the plea of the Constitution that we make the Divine Office what it was originally intended to be: a means of sanctifying the *whole* day. Let us be completely willing to make whatever adjustments may be necessary to pray the various "hours" at the time of day for which each is intended (*cfr*. Par. 88). The Constitution urges this especially in the case of Lauds and Vespers, and calls these "the two hinges on which the daily office turns." These are "to be considered as the chief hours and are to be celebrated as such" (Par. 89). That he pray the one reasonably early in the morning and the other in the evening is not asking too much of even the busiest parish priest. Each of us should try to make Compline really a night prayer. None of us should have any qualms about deferring Matins to any time of the day rather than allowing it to displace Lauds as his morning prayer.

Of course our difficulties with the Breviary are not going to vanish with the new changes. We shall still wish we could pray it more *"attente"* instead of having to answer the phone in the middle of a psalm and losing our place and wondering whether we should start over—or just quit. We shall still wish we could say it more *"devote"* instead of thinking with our minds how dispiriting are our parish problems while saying with our lips how inspiring are God's deeds. But we cannot let this get us down. Here too we need to say to ourselves over and over again: *"Agnoscite quod agitis"*! We cannot remind ourselves too often that when we take up the Divine Office we are the Church in the very act of fulfiling her *first* work: "glorifying You on earth." When we pray the Breviary we are Christ here and now singing his canticle of praise to the Father and pleading for the salvation of men. Our priesthood is this world's noblest witness to man's fumbling effort to love one another as the Lord loved us—let us never cease trying to bring his kind of love to *this* priestly work too.

The recitation of the Divine Office is one of the distinct glories of American priests. Those who have been around tell us that we cede first place to none in our dogged fidelity to the Breviary. As long as we say it in Latin, it is just possible that we American priests say more of it and understand less of it than priests anywhere in the world today!

But does this laudable fidelity stem from an appreciation of prayer or from a fear of the *sub gravi* penalty? What motivates us really: the spirit of worship or the spirit of legalism? The trickery of emphasis must not blind us to the simple truth that, while the Divine Office is indeed the prayer of Christ and public prayer, it can in fact be neither unless, first of all, it is *prayer*. Do you agree with me that with most of us most of the time it is *not* prayer? We "recite the Office" but we do not pray.

This is not completely our fault, nor is it even the fault of the Latin. Reciting the Breviary in a language we know rather than in one we do not know will certainly help. None of you here feels more strongly on this than I. Because I know that the act of prayer is a grace, I regard the use of Latin in prayer a positive hindrance or *"obex"* to divine grace for most of us. I do not subscribe to the theory that we should place unnecessary obstacles in the way of God's grace. There are enough obstacles already to the grace of prayer and I do not see how we can justify retention of the Latin where it is really a hindrance to God's grace in the act of prayer. And I rather suspect that of all the changes to come out of Vatican Council II none will be more widely or more heartily welcomed by priests for purely personal reasons than the opening of the door to the vernacular in the Breviary. But let us be honest: merely changing from Latin to English will not automatically solve our major difficulty with the Divine Office. That "major difficulty" devolves around the problem of prayer and not around the problem of language.

What we need even more than a change in language is a change in attitude. The attitude most of us now have regarding the Breviary is crassly legalistic: it is a *sub gravi* duty to perform rather than a prayer to be prayed. I blame this attitude not on the language but on "the system." I blame it largely on the kind of "conditioning" we got at the outset. For months before subdiaconate my classmates and I were taught three things about the Breviary: first, that its recitation, to be performed in its entirety daily, was henceforth to be a *sub gravi*, official function; second, that its intricate rubrics required both technical skill and minute fidelity; third, that it was great and magnificent prayer. But so much care and study and practice went into the first two that the third somehow never quite sank in. I can honestly say that I was never taught to make *prayer* my first concern when I was introduced to the Breviary. Perhaps my devoted teachers intended that I should make prayer my first concern. Perhaps they took for granted that I had enough sense to make prayer my first concern. But the plain fact is that I did not. I was concerned first about the duty, especially its solemn and frightening *sub gravi* aspect. I was deeply aware that upon my accession to major orders this was to be an "*officium*," a professional duty, incumbent upon me every day for the rest of my life. I was

concerned secondly about the external mechanics of this duty—
about such momentous matters as when to double the antiphons
and how to decode the cryptography of the Ordo. I remember
distinctly being told not to worry too much if the words my lips
formed meant little or nothing to me: I was saying "the prayer of
the Church" and by some mysterious kind of supernatural osmosis
these meaningless nothings my lips so meticulously formed gave
great glory to God. And over the years the same sweet reassurance
came in the annual clergy retreat. What really matters is to "say"
the Breviary—too bad if in the process you make like a parrot
instead of a man, but just wonderful so long as you say it.

O Father, what unconscionable garbage this is! It is past time
everyone of us realize that the Breviary is nothing if it is not prayer.
To pray at all we must pray *as men,* as intelligent beings. The minds
and hearts God gave us must be involved. We are not parrots or
tape-recorders. We are men. There is only one way we can pray,
whether the prayer be private or public, and that is as men. The
curious notion that "public prayer" somehow dispenses us from
acting as rational beings is repulsive to God, whose Son said: "You
hypocrites! It was a true prophecy Isaias made of you when he
said, 'This people does me honor with its lips, but its heart is far
from me.' Their worship of me is vain" (Matt. 15:8). The constitution on the Sacred Liturgy says that "Because it is the public prayer
of the Church, the Divine Office is a source of personal prayer"
(Par. 90). Not only does public prayer not excuse us from making it
personal prayer as well, the Council Fathers said it must be personal
prayer *because* it is public prayer.

The primary fact confronting you and me every time we take up
that book is that *now we must pray*—not that we must perform a
certain duty in a certain way and finish it by a certain time. The
canon lawyers and moral theologians have just about ruined the
Divine Office for us. We have so much to unlearn. The one
relevant truth we must learn is this: to recite the Breviary means that

I must pray. I must pray the *only* way I can: as a man, as a rational being. To be prayer at all it must be a conscious encounter with God. Prayer is a man in the act of talking to God—and because this is a human act, the man who is engaged in it must know and he must mean and, yes, he must feel what he is saying. A meaningless, mechanical recitation is not an *actus religionis* because it is not even an *actus humanus*. This kind of "religion" mocks God, and this kind of "prayer" debases man. It is absolutely and completely phony.

And so we cannot remind ourselves too often that the Divine Office cannot really be the prayer of Christ or the public prayer of the Church unless it is prayer. There is simply no point in talking about the necessity of prayer in the life of the priest unless each and every priest is completely willing to make the one prayer Christ asks of him really a prayer. When I first prepared these remarks I collected loads of quotes from the gospels showing the absolute primacy of prayer in the life of the Eternal Priest. But then I thought "how nice—but how pointless." The Church has given us priests one prayer and one only to pray: her own, Christ's own. Until we are completely willing to take *this* one seriously, *as prayer,* we are tilting at windmills to quote the words and example of the Lord about prayer in general. Our Lord himself has put this prayer in our hands. This one is unique. I am convinced it is a waste of time to talk to priests about the importance of meditation or the rosary or any prayer in their lives until each and everyone of us is in dead earnest about making *this* one real prayer.

How insistent the Constitution on the Sacred Liturgy is on this point. Read through Chapter Four: on the Divine Office. You cannot fail to notice straight off how different it reads from the chapter on the Divine Office in our moral theology manuals. Do you know why it is so different? It changed just one word. Where the moral theology manuals and Canon Law invariably speak of "reciting" the Divine Office, the Constitution speaks of "praying" the Divine Office. The pointed and insistent recurrence of the word "pray" or "prayer" in this chapter so fascinated me that I counted the number of times it is used: a total of twenty-one in only eighteen paragraphs! The phrase "recite the divine office" is used very sparingly, and then only in reference to the obligation. Because prayer depends on grace it is indelicate to talk about an "obligation to pray," and therefore, in the context of strict obligation, the Constitution follows the theology manuals and speaks in terms of "reciting" rather than "praying." But there is one interesting exception: paragraph 96 says, "Clerics not bound to office in choir, if they are in major orders, are *bound to pray* the entire office every day." This is more than interesting, it is astounding! Paragraph 96 covers us—you and me. What make you of this, that you and I are "bound to pray the entire office every day?" Bound not just to recite, but bound to *pray!*

Let me call your attention to something else most interesting in the Constitution's chapter on the Divine Office. Paragraph 84, quoted earlier, says: "When this wonderful song of praise is rightly performed by priests and others . . . deputed by the Church . . . then it is the very prayer which Christ himself addresses to the Father." How significant those two little words and how easily missed: when *rightly* performed, *then* it is the prayer of Christ! The clear implication here is that when it is not rightly performed, when it is hurried and meaningless, then whatever it is it is not the prayer of Christ.

That *prayer* is the crux of the matter becomes obvious in the famous paragraph 101 which makes possible the use of the vernacular in the Divine Office. Prayer is the only consideration in allowing us to use the English. After an accolade to the retention of Latin, the paragraph continues: ". . . but in individual cases the Ordinary has the power of granting the use of the vernacular translation to those clerics for whom the use of Latin constitutes a grave obstacle to their *praying* the office properly." It is only because she wants you to *pray* the Breviary that the Church will allow you the use of your own language. And look you to it: by seeking and using this privilege you commit yourself not just to reciting the Divine Office in English but to *praying* it!

You and I share in the priesthood of Jesus Christ in a unique and exalted way. His highest priestly function was to send his canticle of praise to the Father. How privileged we are to share in this Godly Duty of his—his *Officium Divinum*.

But each of us shares also in his other priestly function: to redeem our brethren. This was his *Officium Humanum*—the Human Office, the saving ministry to mankind, the ministry of charity to his brethren.

Let us, sharers in his priestly office, re-dedicate ourselves to his two-fold *officium* and ours: the *officium divinum* and the *officium humanum caritatis*. Obediently we take us the *officium divinum* daily. And day after day we surrender our very lives to the *officium humanum caritatis*. But let us do so even as he did: "by stealing away from them to pray." The *officium humanum* will remain barren unless we back it up with the *officium divinum*. By word and example he taught us that this *officium humanum* depends on prayer, on being alone regularly in "I-Thou" encounter with the Father. The *officium divinum* is this encounter—if we really pray it. Let us ask for the grace of prayer as we take up the Breviary so that in this "I-Thou" encounter we may seek and find the God who is our Rock, our Shepherd, our Father.

15. "Remember thy last end"

BEFORE I BEGIN a discussion of death, judgment, heaven and hell, may I be permitted an observation or two? Does anybody know where we picked up the slogan "four last things?" And does anybody know how or why we put hell fourth and last? It seems to me that for centuries Christian piety viewed what we now call "the *last* things" rather as a beginning than as an ending. The whole mysticism of "the eighth day," so vigorous and so significant in the early Church, regarded what we now call "last" as a new beginning, as the "new creation." When and where did we adopt this "terminal" attitude that we have today? The birthday, the *dies natalis,* of the martyrs was always the day of their death. Even to this day we count the day of death of a canonized saint as the day of his "birth." Dare we have second thoughts about the wisdom of viewing death as the last anything? As the end? Is this the authentic Christian perspective? True, it serves well to frighten us; but what is it doing over the long haul toward the formation in us of the true Christian spirit?

What ever happened to our Christian consciousness of the *Parousia,* the true end-time? For the Christian this is the one last thing, and who killed it in our modern Catholic piety? Not one Catholic in one hundred knows the meaning of the word. And does anybody know how and why we ever came to coin this slogan in its familiar sequence: death, judgment, heaven and hell? Why, in our grim enumeration of these "last things," did we put hell dead last? Dare we look objectively at this well-worn slogan and in the warm light of Christian hope wonder out loud about the wisdom or the propriety of putting hell last, as though to infer that this is our "last end?"

The good news the New Testament shouts out at you from every page is precisely that those who "believe and are baptized" are destined for heaven as their last end, not for hell. It is we who are called upon to thank God our Father "for making us fit to share the light which saints inherit, for rescuing us from the power of darkness, and transferring us to the kingdom of his beloved Son" (Col. 1:12–13). It is not to hell but to heaven the Mass transports us daily in prophetic anticipation, as with all the heavenly host we cry out with one voice "Holy, holy, holy." And so, with your kind indulgence, I should like to invert the hallowed order ever so slightly and talk about heaven last. After all, I should not like to close this book leaving you in hell! And as we remember the four last things, let us also remember that we are to remember other truths of our Faith first and more often. It is the Old Law which tells you at all times to remember your last end; but it is the Sacrifice of the New Law which tells you to remember the blessed passion, resurrection and ascension of God's Son. Careful always to keep first things first and last things last, let us turn to the meditation at hand.

"What man shall live and not see death," asks the Psalmist. We priests remember death every day. There is a distinct death-consciousness about the whole hour of Compline. *"Noctem quietam et finem perfectam concedat nobis Dominus omnipotens."* Death forms the theme of the *Nunc Dimittis,* underscored in its lovely antiphon with the double-meaning: "Protect us, Lord, while we are awake and safeguard us while we sleep, that we may keep watch with

Christ and *rest in peace*." The Roman Breviary, of course, is neither first nor alone in noting the subtle association between sleep and death—our literature is filled with it. Compline alludes to it again in the Short Response: "Into your hands, O Lord, I commend my spirit." In her own night prayer the Church reminds each of us daily of his own death.

You know, it is strange—this consciousness of your own impending death. All of us, from roughly the age of seven on, are quite aware that it is inevitable, recognizing with the dying Hamlet that "this fell sergeant, death, is strict in his arrest." But there is normally very little real consciousness of it in our earlier years. The healthy, busy young man scarcely every thinks about dying. But as we grow older, when the first classmate dies, whether we be in good health or in bad, the shadow inexorably lengthens. By the time he is forty it is unusual for a man not to advert to his own death at least once every week. You cannot shut out the numbing awareness that steals over you from time to time: 'I wonder how much longer now! Under the best of statistical circumstances my life here is now at least one-half over—two-thirds over—three-fourths over."

There is a shattering line at the end of Hamlet which has to be heard and seen for the full impact. The Prince, with the deadly poison fast at work in his body, lies mortally stricken in the arms of his friend. This is what he says: "O, I could tell you—but let it be. I am dead, Horatio." Hamlet has ten more lines to say before the end of the play; he is yet to struggle with Horatio and summon strength enough to wrest the poisoned cup away from him. All this *after* he has said, "I am dead, Horatio." We are like Hamlet, except that he knew it and sometimes we do not. We are all of us dying men—even the youngest and healthiest among us. We still have our allotted lines to say; certain struggles still lie ahead. But often the cause of death is already at work within us: a few undetected cancerous cells, an artery that is ever so gradually closing shut. "I am dead, Horatio."

And surely we are all aware of the inexplicable but statistically notorious fact: because we are priests chances are pretty good that we shall die suddenly and alone. There is a certain natural finality too about the death of a priest which cannot escape us: most men know that, in a sense, they live on after death in their children— but we have kept our children in our loins. We leave no ancestries behind when we die. There is nothing quite as dead as a dead priest.

There is nothing wrong about hating death. This may prove a bit futile, but it certainly is not wrong. Jesus hated death. He recoiled in bloody sweat from his own death. Three times that we know of, he kicked death in the teeth by bringing deceased persons back to life. Of course he hated death—he hated sin, and is death not the work of sin? St. Paul seems to use the two words death and sin interchangeably. God did not make death. Satan did. Why should we Christians not hate death? There is nothing Christian in the pious pose that we are expected somehow to like or welcome death itself, any more than that we are expected to like and welcome sickness as such. Our Christian faith tells us that sickness and death are punishment, and nobody except a pervert *likes* punishment. Where did we ever get the phony idea that, as Christians, we are supposed to look kindly upon death? Indeed the acceptance of death in a spirit of detachment from self and of utter surrender to God is a magnificently Christian thing; it is, in fact, the Christian's great and final act of faith which embarks him on his return to the Father. But we must not confuse the *acceptance* of death with death itself. The one is a great grace; the other is a curse and a penalty to be feared and resisted.

"It is appointed unto men once to die, and after death comes the judgment," says the author of Hebrews (9:27). The judgment which preoccupies us is, of course, the "particular judgment." This, inevitably, is the one to which we refer in the "four last things." Under the influence of Greek thought with its dichotomy between body and soul, and colored heavily by nineteenth-century individualism, the particular judgment has assumed a frightening centrality in our modern Catholic consciousness. It is frightening not only because it is so definitive, but also because it projects each of us into such stark naked aloneness. Let us thank God for the grace of this insight into revelation for, when all else fails, this may be the only motive force powerful enough to scare us back onto track.

But I wonder how genuinely Christian this is. Fear is unquestionably salutary, yet I cannot rid my mind of St. Paul's assurance that because we are sons and no longer slaves we are not "to be governed by fear." Even the Old Testament called upon the Lord God: "Be not a terror to me, you are my hope in the day of affliction" (Jer. 17:17). Our nightmarish preoccupation with the particular judgment has not only confirmed us in our questionable fixation regarding the "salvation of the *soul*" (and the individual, isolated soul at that), but has completely obstructed that exhilarating Christian vision of the end-time, the *Parousia*. If we think of the "general judgment" at all, we think of it as merely consequential— nothing more than a kind of public ratification of the particular judgment. The "resurrection of the body" in which we profess our faith in the Apostles' Creed concerns us but little. We are quite anxious about saving our souls, but we stop there. The Lord Christ did not come to save *your soul*, he came to save *you*. And our view of the Redemption is really quite self-centered: we regard salvation not only in terms of *the* soul but of *my* soul. The authentic Christian hope of a *mankind* resurrected and returned to the Father in the definitive kingdom of the Princely Son holds little meaning or attraction for us. Jesus Christ did not come to lead souls to heaven; he came to lead all men to heaven. The particular judgment is not the final chapter either in your redemption or in the Redemption. Baptism and the *Parousia* form the two terms of our redemption— not yours or mine but *ours*. Let us indeed remember the particular judgment. Let us have a healthy fear of the particular judgment.

But let our communal hope in the communal glory of the end-time light our way.

Hell exists. Even though hell is mentioned more than one-hundred times in the Old Testament, our doctrine of hell is really a Christian revelation. Jesus—the gentle, forgiving, merciful Jesus who loved us enough to die for us—he it was who revealed the real existence of the real hell to the world. Hell is punishment: eternal punishment which includes fire.

Father, have you ever thought this about hell: never was a greater blow struck for the freedom of the human will! No higher or more frightening vindication of man's freedom exists than the doctrine of hell—to *this* degree is man free; to *this* extent is he accountable!

Even though Sacred Scripture assures you that you have been "marked out for eternal life" by God's call at baptism, you *can* lose it. You were not *given* everlasting life at baptism, you were *promised* it. And there was a hook to the promise. It was a *conditioned* promise: "If it is life you wish to enter, keep the commandments." You were rescued from Satan at your baptism, but you are free to return to him. There are no chains in the kingdom of heaven. You renounced Satan, but you are free to repudiate the repudiation. There are turn-coats in the kingdom of heaven. True, you are sustained en route by hope. But remember that hope, withal, is only hope. It is neither certainty nor possession. If it were either it could not be hope. While hope is not a reed shaken in the wind, it does of its very nature admit the possibility of non-fulfillment.

It pays to remember too that, whatever the theological debates about the interrelations of grace and merit, there is no debate in two cases: it is *de fide* that two graces you cannot truly merit— and they are the two that really count: first grace and last grace. You cannot earn or merit the grace of final perseverance. Because there is no way for you infallibly to guarantee the last grace, the possibility of hell is a perennial sword of Damocles over your head. This dogma that the grace of final perseverance cannot be in-

fallibly merited is a most interesting bit of theology. What it boils
down to is the touching revelation of the omnipotent God respect-
fully awaiting the decisions of your free will, right up to the very
last second. There are no chains in the kingdom of heaven! What
a magnificent but sobering deference to your freedom, this dogma
that you cannot merit the grace of final perseverance? Right to the
very end God respects your freedom of choice. He refuses to restrict
that freedom by commiting you ahead of time to final perseverance!
How magnificent this divine deference to your human freedom.
Yes, and how sobering its implications! Right up to the last
moment you are completely free to turn from God your Father who
"rescued you from the powers of darkness and transferred you into
the kingdom of his beloved Son." You are free to return to sin
and to Satan whom you renounced with such a flourish at your
baptism. The freedom to make this choice is yours right up to the
end, solely and exclusively yours. Because God made you free, the
freedom to choose hell is yours right up to the very last. And this is
why you cannot merit the grace of final perseverance.

Now there are two things you must remember about hell: it was
not made for you, and you were not made for it. Hell is not your
destiny; it is not your last end. You have been "marked out for
eternal life." "God himself," said St. John, "has made us a promise,
the promise of eternal life" (I John 2:26). He made this promise
to you when he adopted you at your baptism. He reiterates it and
reconfirms it every time he encounters you in a sacrament. He
attached a special warranty to it by singling you out and calling you
to the priesthood. True, you *can* choose to go to hell. But your direction and your bearing is heaven. Have no doubt about it: you are
"in via salutis"(I Cor. 1:18). It is only by deliberate detour, only by
premeditated derailment, that you can go to hell. God himself has
not only made the promise of eternal life to you, he has reconfirmed
that promise again and again. What about this? Does it have no
meaning? "God keeps faith. God will not play you false"—four

times St. Paul uses these very words (I Cor. 1:9, I Cor. 10:12, II Cor. 1:18, II Thess. 3:3). How significant this is! "It is God himself who called you to share in the life of his Son . . . and God keeps faith" (I Cor. 1:9). Father, is it not monstrous to suppose that God, after doing all he has done to signify your election, would capriciously rub it all out by refusing you the last grace, the grace of final perseverance? "God keeps faith . . . He will not play you false." Have no doubt about it: you can count on him. "God will strengthen your resolution to the last" (I Cor. 1:8).

There is really only one uncertainty: can he count on you? The dogma that you cannot merit the final grace bespeaks no reluctance on the part of God to give it. Certainly in your own case God has gone about as far as he can to indicate that he wants to give it and that he will give it. This dogma simply shows the amazing respect God has for your freedom.

Before you start worrying too much, however, about how you are going to use that precious freedom of yours, remember this: with perfect foreknowledge of how you would use your freedom, God *did* call you, he *did* make you the promise of eternal life. He *has* repeatedly reconfirmed that promise. Take heart, Father! God does not mock. He has not been teasing. He acts in earnest. "God keeps faith . . . He will not play you false." Remember the assurance given you by God's Spirit through the Apostle Paul: "He has chosen us out, in Christ, to be saints . . . marking us out beforehand (so his will decreed) to be his adopted children through Jesus Christ" (Eph. 1:4-5). "All those who from the first were known to God, he has destined from the first to be molded into the image of his Son . . . So predestined, he called them; so called, he justified them; so justified, he glorified them" (Rom. 8:29-30). Friday, in the hour of None, the God who called you and made a covenant with you at baptism, reminds you of his faithfulness in his own words: "I have entered into a covenant with my chosen one . . . I will not withdraw my grace from him, nor will I default on my word; I will not violate the covenant I made, nor will I alter the promise of my lips." Father, underline these verses in Psalm 88, and take heart in their assurance any Friday you pray the hour of None.

Why do we insist on being so diffident about heaven? Perhaps we think it poor form to appear confident. The Church, you know, has no such qualms. When she will enact the Rite of Christian Burial over your mortal remains, she will all but flaunt her confidence that your soul has gone to heaven and that your body will too. Have you ever taken a good close look at the burial liturgy? It is an amazing thing. What rich material for meditation! I suggest that some day when you have thirty minutes you open the Roman Missal and the Ritual and just read and drink in the message there set forth. And if you want a "*compositio loci*" for your meditation don't make it Joe Blow's funeral, make it *yours,* for these prayers the Church is sooner or later going to say for you over your mortal remains.

The patent assumption is that your priestly soul has gone to heaven. Notice the tense: not "is going to go"—HAS GONE! The macabre "Purgatory obsession" under whose spell we labor today, wherever it came from, certainly did not come from here. Purgatory is not so much as mentioned or even hinted at in the Catholic burial liturgy. There are several allusions to the possibility of hell— but they are quickly and decisively brushed aside. One discordantly jarring note in the Rite is the *Dies Irae*—that overly-long, overly-grim, overly-boring sequence of the Funeral Mass. But this is a rather late encrustment which had been originally written and used as the sequence of the Mass for the First Sunday of Advent and its gospel reading on the end of the world. Because the Constitution on the Sacred Liturgy has ordered a reform of the burial rities to "express more clearly the paschal character of Christian death," we can now hope for the early burial of the *Dies Irae* itself and look forward to hearing no more of those painful renditions of this Gregorian masterpiece by inept choirs.

Even in its present unreformed form, most of our liturgy is an unabashed rhapsody of hope. The trust of this hope is particularly strong in the special Collect, Secret and Post-Communion *"pro defuncto sacerdote"*—those the celebrant will chant at *your* funeral Mass: ". . . *in caelesti regno, Sanctorum tuorum jubeas jungi consortio* . . ." Note the recurrence throughout the Rite of the key words "light" and "life." "I am the resurrection and the life . . . We give you thanks, O Lord, holy Father, almightly and everlasting God, through Christ our Lord in whom the hope of a blessed resurrection has shone upon us . . . To your faithful, O Lord, life is only changed, not taken away; and when the house of this life on earth has been destroyed an eternal home is prepared in heaven. Therefore, together with the angels and archangels . . . and the whole host of the heavenly army, we sing the hymn of your glory: Holy, Holy, Holy . . ." (I have always thought the *Sanctus* of the Mass on the day of burial the most relevant and beautiful of all, for this one, in a special way, is the fulfilment of what we only anticipate in the *Sanctus* of any other Mass.) And then that exultant soaring song, sung by your Mother the Church, as you, priest of God, are borne out of God's holy temple for this last time: *"In paradisum deducant te angeli."* You exit on a note of triumph. However you in life may have doubted, the Church here makes no secret of her irrepressible hope: she has gotten you home!

Father, on this happy note we conclude our discussions. Please understand that this "happy note" is not wishful thinking. It is not cheap sentiment or false religious euphoria. It is firmly grounded on God's love, on God's fidelity. It lives on your hope. It is what that beautiful prayer to the Holy Spirit means in saying: "Grant . . . that we may always rejoice in his holy comfort." You *are* going to heaven. God has called you there, and God keeps faith. This is your destiny. This is your birthright. This is your true home. "I am going to prepare a place for you (in my Father's house where there are many mansions), so that where I am you also may be . . . I am the way . . . No man comes to the Father except through me."

Father, rise above your fears and your doubts. Be neither of little faith nor of little hope. "God himself has made you a promise, the promise of eternal life. He will strengthen your resolution to the last." He is the faithful God. He will not play you false. Just you keep your eye on the ball. Keep your sights set on target. Keep the goal in view. Take a page from the book of another priest of another day who said: "Forgetting what I have left behind, intent on what lies before me, I press on with the goal in view, eager for the prize: God's heavenly summons in Christ Jesus. All of us who are fully grounded must be of this mind . . . we find our true home in heaven . . ." (Philippians 3:13–14, 20).

Father, I pray that this blessed hope, virile and constant, may be the lamp unto your priestly feet until the end of your days.